Good Mom Rules:

Ditch Mom Guilt
&
Find Your Happy

Alysia Lyons

Authentic Endeavors Publishing/Wellness Book Endeavors

Interior Design by Amit Dey

Good Mom Rules
ISBN: 978-1-955668-79-8 (Paperback)
ISBN: 978-1-955668-81-1 (Ebook)

Library of Congress Control Number: 2023917779

I dedicate this book to my son, Zander, who changed my life forever for the better the day he was born. I am so happy and proud to be your mom.

And to my Life Coach, Michelle Moore. I owe this beautiful human much more than I could ever repay. She gave me the gift of guilt-free motherhood, and I have a better connection with Zander because of her passion for human healing.

Acknowledgments

I interviewed over 50 moms before, during, and after writing this book. Thank you for your time, vulnerability, honesty, and trust. I changed the names of the moms I mentioned in the book to respect your privacy. Without you, there would be no book. Thank you sincerely.

Mom, thank you for being my mom. I know you think you could have done better, but you contributed to making me the woman I am, and you did a wonderful job!

Thank you, Shannah, for your ferocious curiosity, and your beautiful mind knows all the grammar rules I'll never be able to remember.

Coach Sean Smith, you introduced me to this coaching world. Had I known then what I know now about how meeting you would change my life, I would have done it sooner, with more focused intent, and paid much more. I learned most of the tools I shared in this book from you, and I thank you for that, as well as all you've done and continue to do in the world.

Zander, thank you for picking me to be your mom. I love you with all my heart and soul. You gave me new life when you were born. You've helped me course correct many times. I can't wait to see the amazing man you will become, and don't you dare grow up too fast!

Last but not least, thank you, Larry, for all your love and support. Thank you for always being encouraging even when you don't necessarily believe in my vision. I love our talks and that you are not afraid to share your soul and your life with me.

There are many people I want to thank, but if I shared them all by name, it would probably add another 500 pages to this book. Thank you to all those who have supported me along the way.

Table of Contents

Foreword

$\mathcal{B}$ ad. *Terrible. Unworthy. Inferior. Lazy. Uncaring.*

These nasty, horrible little words are things we utter to ourselves daily.

This seems to be the trend with motherhood.

We live in an age of social media burden, and as moms, we love to beat ourselves up over our shortcomings, and in that, we turn to the common phrase, "mom guilt."

The first time I experienced mom guilt was when I was in early labor with my firstborn because my liver was shutting down, and it was no longer safe for her to be in utero. Wow, way to start parenting off right with an early eviction notice because your body hates your child [facepalm]. And since then, I've felt guilty for things like yelling when I'm under stress, not wanting to play with them when I'm tired, letting them eat McDonald's chicken nuggets after a long day…the list could go on forever.

But here's the problem with the trendy feeling of mom guilt: It doesn't serve you or help you become the mother you are ultimately destined to be.

Motherhood isn't about carrying the burden of guilt but learning from the situation and growing.

As a favor, I agreed to read and edit this book for my friend and colleague, but it actually turned out to be a favor for myself. With real-life anecdotes and tangible lessons, I now realize I can take that mom guilt, release it, and use the lesson as a steppingstone for growth as the mom I'm truly meant to be and who my daughters and son need.

Alysia has survived and conquered the mom guilt through realization and acceptance, and we can all take a page from her book (literally).

Mompreneur and total #bossbabe, she's pushed through a divorce, has conquered multiple surrogacies, survived terrible circumstances with her son, escalated in the writing world, and has flourished in the motherhood role, all because she has learned to realize, accept, and release the guilt that burdens us all.

Motherhood is flipping HARD, and guilt comes naturally. It sticks to you and begins to change who you are meant to be. Do yourself a favor and grab a notebook before starting this book. Diving into who you are and why you harbor your guilt will help with your realization and release as Alysia walks you through the process.

Good Moms Don't is truly the real-world application of overcoming the struggles of motherhood one truth at a time and developing that emotional intelligence that we are never taught.

If you've opened this book, you're already a great mother. Now it's time for you to realize it.

Lisa Autry
Founder & CEO
The Daughter Diaries, Inc.

Author of *The Real Moms Playbook*
TheDaughterDiary.com
Instagram: @thedaughterdiaries

I Want to be a Good Mom

My y son was around two years old the first time I was called a bad mom. When I became a single mom, I searched for additional avenues of income to allow me to work from home. I found an ad to become a surrogate, and I knew it was something I wanted to do. Since having Zander, who is currently eleven, I've been a surrogate for three international mothers.

During my first journey, I started contracting at 30 weeks, and my doctor put me on strict bed rest. I suddenly needed someone to take care of my then two-year-old Zander. The only person available to help full-time was my friend Amanda, who lived 45 minutes away. I stayed with her for the first few days, but my contractions kept coming. I ended up in the hospital while doctors tried to stop me from going into labor. After the contractions stopped, the doctors treated me for pneumonia I contracted there.

When they released me a week later, Amanda and I decided Zander should stay with her, and she would bring him to visit me on weekends. We did this for about a month until my doctor cleared me, and I returned to care for him.

About six months after I delivered the first surrogate baby, I was about to start contracts to do it again for another mother when a girl messaged me. She was Amanda's friend, and when I told her I would be a surrogate again, she laid into me. She told me I was a *terrible* mom for letting another person care for my son. Not a bad mom. A terrible mom. There is nothing worse you could say to me. Even if I am 99% sure I'm doing a good job, there's still the 1% I question.

Within a year of the conversation, Child Protective Services took her two children from her because of neglect. Her son was malnourished, unwashed, and her home was full of dog feces and dirty diapers. It amazed me how someone like *her* had the nerve to judge me for circumstances out of my control. And yes, I judged her right back.

One of the reasons I wrote this book was because of the judgment moms show each other. And I know I do it, too. Here are a few you might have heard: If you stay at home, you're riding the gravy train to lazy town. If you work a job, you should be ashamed for letting someone else raise your kids. Women who have C-sections aren't real moms, nor are those who use IVF or adopt. If you breastfeed, you're better than those who use a bottle but don't do it publicly, heaven forbid, because we might see a breast.

Raising kids is difficult enough without the pressure we put on each other and ourselves to be a *good mom*. Truthfully, the pressure that seems to come from others is from an internal source. We see pictures of other moms in real life or on social media doing something we wish we could do, and because we can't or don't, we beat ourselves up for not being better.

I'm not saying mom-shaming doesn't happen. It does. Remember the "What's your excuse, Mom?" She posted a picture of herself surrounded by her three kids, each under three, and she had a seemingly perfect body. The post went viral in 2013, and many moms, including me, felt fat shamed. I understand she wanted to inspire mothers to get into shape and not use their children as an excuse, but it felt like an attack. In 2018, she recreated the infamous picture but changed the tagline to "What's your reason?" The updated version sends a much better message, and I feel more inspired to get healthy *for* my son. Bravo!

I've been called a bad mom a few other times since the encounter with the unfit mother. While going through a divorce, his dad threatened to take custody of our son because he thought I was doing a bad job. Truthfully though, I've probably called myself worse things than anyone else. Unless those words come out of their mouth, no one calls you a bad mom. Assuming someone thinks it is *not* the same as them calling you a bad mom. You don't have access to their thoughts. It is your *own* judgment projected onto them.

Over the last few years, I've worked on that critical voice and concentrated on what type of mom I want to be. My temper has improved. I've slowed down my reaction time when I'm angry. And if I explode, I will explain why. Every time. It has become part of our relationship, our bond.

A few months ago, my life coach gave me an assignment to get to know the type of person I wanted to help in my coaching business. He said to get to know them and what they struggle with. Find out about their struggles, and you will figure out how to help them. I interviewed dozens of mothers- those working outside the home, homemakers, single, married, new, experienced, and empty-nesters− and noticed a pattern. I heard their guilt. Once I noticed a theme of the calls, I started to ask them directly, "Do you ever feel like a bad mom?"

The answer is usually "Yes!" or "Of course!" and even *"All* the time!"

Knowing I'm not the only one beating myself up is devastating. Many women hold onto guilt and shame about the type of mom they are (because others do it better) or things they wish they had handled differently (because beating yourself up is how we change the past, right?). We love to judge ourselves through our current perspective. Meanwhile, we *must go through the past to* become who we are today. We must make mistakes to learn from and grow.

My purpose for this book is to help moms release their guilt, live in the present moment, heal their relationship with the past, start practicing self-care, and create happier and peace-filled lives.

For *years*, I felt like I was doing a bad job. I beat myself up for things I judged as wrong. How did I not know better? Do better? Where was my crystal ball to tell me I was making a wrong decision? Why am I not more like this woman or that one? How come I'm not more like my mom? Amid all my guilt, Zander saw me as only a child can. In his eyes, I could do no wrong. "You are the sun, and I revolve around you." That is a direct quote from him at age four. I call those #Zandersations on Facebook.

My goal is to help you understand guilt. What is it? Where does it come from? I also want to help you let go of whatever you hold on to in order to live in the moment. When you're beating yourself up for things you did or didn't do, you're not fully in the present. If you're living in the past, you're missing the beauty of your kids at this age. They grow up fast! I blinked, and Zander turned eleven. I look at Facebook memories and think, "Where did my baby go?"

You are a good mom despite and because of your mistakes. If you *weren't* a good mom, you wouldn't worry about being one. You wouldn't be beating yourself up. You wouldn't be reading this book. Bad moms don't think they are bad. They think everyone else is to blame for how their children behave, and they are primarily concerned with themselves.

We, as parents, are our children's greatest teachers, and there are lessons they can only learn from us. Some of those lessons come from the mistakes we make. When we stay stuck in a cycle of self-abuse, we rob ourselves of the joy our children bring us. And our babies don't get the happy moms they deserve.

In the following chapters, I share some of the rules moms try to live by and use to hold themselves to impossible standards. Some were mine, and some came from the moms I interviewed. I hope that my examples and tools will teach you how to ditch mom guilt and find your happy.

What is Guilt, and How is it Created?

$\mathcal{B}$efore becoming a Life Coach, I didn't understand guilt or how it was created. Honestly, I'd never given much thought to it at all. I had no idea how heavy the guilt I carried around was. You can't know how freeing it is to let it go until you do. But imagine holding a beach ball underwater. When you release it, it flies up into the air like a rocket. That's what it feels like to be free of this burdensome emotion. It can manifest in your life as self-punishment, self-condemnation, and self-abuse. And none of those sound like fun.

How is guilt created? Guilt is created when our actions conflict with our beliefs. Deep down, we all want to be good people. We need to believe we are. We have an idea of what that means, and we create moral rules to maintain our identity. For example, a well-known moral rule is that a good person doesn't steal. If we break one of these rules, we punish ourselves - just like those who break a law in the criminal justice system receive a punishment. The way we punish ourselves for breaking our moral rules is guilt. When you feel guilty, you relive the situation repeatedly, which takes up a lot of mental energy and can ultimately affect your self-worth and self-esteem.

We also have many roles in our lives. Not only do we want to be a good person, but we also want to be a good woman, mother, friend, etc. Each of these is part of our identity, and rules are contained inside each one. As a mother, you have conscious and unconscious rules to follow in order to think of yourself as a good mom. There are many places we could be getting these rules. We grow up with our parents as examples. Depending on how we feel about our upbringing, we may do what our moms did. Others had a negative childhood experience, and they looked for other examples of what a good mom is. I have my mom on a pedestal. She can do no wrong in my eyes; therefore, I want to be like her. She felt the same about her mom, and neither of us felt we could live up to our role models.

The way to release yourself from guilt is to stop violating the good mom rule. The tricky thing is, most of the time, the actions creating guilt are in the past. Since time travel only exists in movies, that poses a huge problem. We often can't stop the behavior violating our good mom rule. For example, "good moms don't work outside the home" could be your rule. But what if you want to? Or have to? Then what?

If your rule is "good moms don't work outside the home," and you do, in order to release yourself from guilt, you must find an exception to the rule. What reason does a mom work outside the home? Maybe they want to or need to. The good news is that there is an exception to every rule. You just need to give yourself permission to find it.

Guilt is a nasty emotion. The term "mom guilt" sounds kind of cute, like it's not a big deal. I see it carried around like a badge of honor in some cases. "I'm a good mom. Look how guilty I feel." But it's not serving you or your relationship with your children. If left unchecked, it can suck the joy from motherhood. It can create an emotional disconnection between you and your kids. Because of my guilt, I started emotionally disconnecting from Zander to protect myself from future resentment. More than likely, I created the thing I feared by distancing myself from him. It was a lose-lose situation...until I got help.

Conquering your guilt will deepen your self-compassion, self-acceptance, and self-love. Allowing guilt to go unchecked can block you from joy, disconnect you from the present moment and even cause you to self-sabotage. It often creates unexpressed anger, which leads to rage.

As you read this book, I want you to be compassionate with yourself. I bet you never intentionally do anything to hurt your children. We make choices hoping for the best with the information we have at the time. Like me, I am sure you were not issued a crystal ball when your kids were born. Sometimes we say and do things that don't have the outcome we wanted, and then we feel guilty.

You may not want to forgive yourself for some things you hold on to. I understand. I didn't want to forgive myself either. But releasing this emotion is not condoning the behavior. Forgiving yourself doesn't mean you're happy you did it. It's simply saying, "Okay, I understand how someone in this situation could have done what they did." You just happen to be that person.

Compassion is something we tend to show others more easily. The way we beat ourselves up for the things we've done is far worse than others would expect of us. The things we ruthlessly punish ourselves for are often something we wouldn't even give our kids a consequence for. And we punish ourselves for *years!*

Realistically, you won't stop creating guilt altogether. That's not the goal. I still feel guilty sometimes about most of the topics I address. For example, a few hours before writing this chapter, I spoke with my life coach about feeling bad for working during Zander's Christmas vacation. The difference is that now I do not let it control my life. I use the tools in this book to show grace to myself.

It is possible to stop letting guilt control your life and suck the joy from the present moment. I want this for you and your kids.

Letting go of G.U.I.L.T.

---

*I*f you're experiencing mom guilt (and I've only had two moms ever tell me they don't have any), it's a bigger deal than you know. Guilt is a form of punishing yourself for doing something **wrong**. We spend weeks, months, and *years* beating ourselves up for things that don't deserve that kind of punishment.

What can we do? Let's start by defining *What is a good mom?*

Take some time to answer the question. What does a good mom *do?* If we don't **define** what a good mom does, then it becomes this mystic, unattainable thing we can never live up to. But we have something tangible to attain when we create a clear definition.

For me, good moms love their children. They do whatever it takes to be the best version of themselves. They continue to learn and improve if they fall short of what they feel they should be. They forgive themselves for not knowing what they didn't know and do their best to change the future instead of the past.

It's clear that I value personal development. I value forgiving myself for not knowing better, and then I do what I can to know better. I struggled with being an angry mom. I wrote about losing my temper in several blogs on my site. For the most part, I can keep my temper under control. And if I have a stronger reaction than is appropriate for the situation, I have a conversation with Zander about it. I will tell him what was going on in my mind, and I apologize. I'll even explain how we can avoid this situation in the future. After the discussion, I will sit with myself and assess where I possibly lack self-care. When I properly care for myself, I am less likely to explode.

I want to encourage you to focus on things you can control. If you think, "Good moms stay at home with their kids," and you have to or *want* to work, that's not something you can control easily. There are things you can do to be a stay-at-home mom (such as a home-based business), but you must act toward that goal. Beating yourself up over not being home with your kids is part of a pattern of self-abuse that doesn't serve you.

Over the last few years, talking about mom guilt, I started creating tools for moms to help them with their guilt. A Mom G.U.I.L.T. Less Toolbox, if you will. Guilt is an acronym for Generosity, Understanding, Integrity, Love, and Trust. In this chapter, I will break down each of the tools into three components, and at any given time, if you feel guilty, you can check in with the toolbox to see if any of your thirty tools need tweaking.

Be generous to yourself.

By nature, women are generous (people in general, but I'm focusing on women). Yes, we often experience women who aren't generous, but I believe those women have deep wounds they haven't addressed. That is not our natural state.

I want to look at generosity from a mom's perspective. When my son needs a drink of water, where does he get that from? My water cup. When we have three hamburger patties, and one is slightly more burned than the others, who gets that one? Me.

Generosity toward our children comes naturally, but I want to encourage you to be generous with yourself.

Self-care gets talked about *plenty* on social media and personal development arenas, and you might be tired of hearing about it, but are you doing it? How do you practice self-care?

One of my self-care practices involves my boundaries. I let my son drink out of my cup, but when I start tracking my water intake by how many cups I drink, I let him know he needs to get his own cup to drink from. That might seem small, but when we aren't setting *and* enforcing our boundaries, we tell our subconscious that we don't matter. And if we don't matter, our self-esteem takes a hit.

A client of mine tagged me in a post on her Instagram with the caption, "Yes, at last! I get to relax in my bathtub with my glass of wine and read my book, 'Good Mom Rules.' Thank you, @ momsupportcorner."

This is what self-care looks like to this mom of ten kids. And I'm not about to say, "If she can do it with ten kids, how come you can't find the time with two?" or something that would make you feel like you're doing a bad job. You are not in the same situation as her. You might not even have a bathtub or don't like baths! Self-care isn't about doing what others do to take care of themselves. Self-care is about how you take care of yourself.

You may have heard or thought, **"Self-care is selfish!** "

Positive Affirmation for Moms: Taking time for myself is not only okay but necessary.

We've probably all heard the analogy that in an airplane when the oxygen mask drops, you put yours on first, and then you help others. Since that is an overused analogy (although still a good one), I'll give you a different one I heard from my friend. Wolves are a fitting example of "take care of yourself first." The alpha male and female in a wolf pack eat first. They eat the liver because it is the most nutrient-dense part of an animal. As a mom, you're the alpha female in your wolf pack. Self-care is essential.

I heard an interview on the RISE Podcast in or around 2020 with Elizabeth Gilbert, author of Eat, Pray, Love. Rachel Hollis and Elizabeth discuss the idea that "self-care is selfish" or "doing something for yourself is selfish." It's used to keep women from "stepping out of place." We are often shamed into staying in line by being told what we are doing is selfish. Perhaps instead, we start to realize that the things we do for ourselves help us feel more fulfilled.

It's *okay* if you believe your purpose on this planet involves more than being someone's mom. We are showing our kids, by our example, how to lead happier, more productive lives.

Being a mom can often feel like you're in a boss battle (that's a video game reference if you or your kids aren't gamers (I'm sure many YouTube videos can explain it). And when you're in a boss battle, you must be at full strength to win.

Be generous with your love.

The next part of generosity for your mom's guilt toolbox is being generous with your love. My son was slightly over a year old when I became a single mom. For a long time, I struggled with the balance between being his friend and being his autocratic disciplinarian.

When I was growing up, my parents divorced. They both remarried when I was four; I remember only bits and pieces of the time my parents were single parents. I was not super into personal development at the time, and I decided I had to be an autocratic disciplinarian who would impose the rules instead of someone who would teach my child skills and lessons. If I was his friend, how could I get him to listen to me when I needed to discipline him? (I learned a lot and began to change my approach on this when Zander was six and I read a parenting book, called No-Drama Discipline written by Daniel J. Siegel, M.D. and Tina Payne Bryson, Ph.D.)

The problem with my approach was that by deciding to be the autocratic disciplinarian in his life, I stopped being the nurturer I am at my core. Taking care of people is what I love to do. Not only was I not being true to who I am, I was depriving my son, Zander, of the love he needed.

My first blog post (although not the first one I published) was called "What Is Your Child's Love Language?" If you aren't familiar with Gary Chapman's book, The 5 Love Languages, he explains there are 5 ways we show love. The way we show love is typically the way we experience love.

One day I realized my dad and I had different love languages, which was one of the reasons I felt he didn't love me. I asked Zander what I do that makes him feel the most loved. He said when I snuggled him. At the time, I did that as infrequently as possible (for many reasons, one of which was my mom guilt).

There's power in understanding your love language as well as asking your child what theirs is. And once you know how they feel most loved by you, do it as much as possible. As my son has gotten older, he still loves his snuggles, but he also likes when I do things for him. I still snuggle with him every morning, and I do plenty of things for him too. I want him to become more self-sufficient, so I sprinkle, "You can do that yourself." Finding balance is key.

I encourage you to ask your children what their love language is. I recently asked Zander if he felt he was getting enough love. We had a beautiful conversation about how he was feeling, and I believe it strengthened our bond.

As humans, one of our deepest wounds is not feeling loved. As moms, we love our children more than anything, and for some (maybe most), actions speak louder than words. Because many of the "mistakes" we make in life stem from that feeling of "I'm not enough" or "I'm not loveable," let's do everything in our power to give our children a full cup of "I *am* enough" and "I *am* loved/loveable."

Be generous with your time.

The third way is to be generous with your time. This one is something many moms might push back on. Do I believe time grows on trees?

No, I don't. And I won't tell you we all have the same 24 hours daily, just figure it out. A single mom working two or more jobs to support her family doesn't have the same 24 hours I do. And if you are that single mom, I honor you for your commitment to do whatever you must to support your family. There are many seasons in our lives. This one won't last forever.

For everyone else, my question is, do we have time, or do we make time? Most of us waste way more time than we realize just because we don't know how to prioritize the time we do have.

As someone who is multi-passionate, has multiple growing businesses, a son, and a large family is at the top of my priority list, I learned how to manage my time. Things needing my attention got it, and other things didn't fall through the cracks.

If optimizing your time is something you want (or need) to do, I suggest you start by writing everything you do over a few days. Just like when you're trying to lose weight, you need to see what you're eating, and writing it down will help you do less mindless eating. We all have time wasters in our day that could get cut out if we chose. Each of us has priorities, whether they are clear to us or not. These are the things that are important to us. If your kids are your top priority, our time with them should reflect that.

I am not saying spend 24 hours a day with your kids. That is unrealistic and not healthy for most people. Quality of time with kids is significantly more influential than quantity.

Look at your day and create a routine, including spending quality time with your kids. Find things you enjoy doing together. Do something that interests them.

Amy McCready, Founder & President of Positive Parenting Solutions, calls this Mind, Body & Soul time. Spend at least 10 minutes a day with each of your kids doing something *they* want to do with you; 1 on 1 can benefit their self-esteem.

Understand your child's choice.

I heard a story a few years ago of a grief counselor who had a dream amidst a deep depression she was in. You see, one day, she woke up next to her husband, approximately age 32, who had died in his sleep. She grieved deeply for her husband, using drugs and alcohol to cope with his loss.

In her dream, she saw her soul sitting in God's weighting room (such a cute concept to me). God asked for volunteers to teach people how to grieve, and her soul volunteered. Next, God asked, "Who wants to teach her how to grieve?" and her husband's soul volunteered.

This story gives me chills, and one of the reasons is that it puts me back at choice in my life. If my soul chose the path my life would take, then the things in my life that used to make me feel like a victim were suddenly things my soul chose.

This might sound a bit "woo woo," but stick with me here. If my soul chose my parents, chose my mission in life, then everything that felt like it "happened to me" and things that felt out of my control were still my choice. My soul chose them because there are lessons inside those situations. These lessons will enable me to help others on their path who struggle with the same thing.

What does this have to do with being a mom and mom guilt?

I believe your children chose *you* to be their mother. I believe there is something they are supposed to learn from you to fulfill their purpose in life. And some of the lessons they will learn will come from your **mistakes** (you know, those things you beat yourself up for?).

One of the things I felt guilty about was divorcing my son's father. I was about a year old when my parents divorced, and I didn't want that for him. I decided to leave when he was fourteen months old, and the cycle repeated. One thing I didn't know then was that my son was now the third generation (at least) to grow up without a father in the home. That's not what I wanted for Zander. And that's not something I want for my future grandkids.

But the thing is, there are lessons Zander is learning from his dad and I being separate, as well as things he learns from my fiancé, Larry being in his life that he wouldn't have learned had I stayed married to his dad.

In the first draft of this book, I mentioned the concept of children choosing their parents, and one of my friends got upset when she read it. She had less-than-perfect parents and didn't particularly like the idea that she chose them. I took it out of the book because it wasn't necessary for what I was trying to communicate at the time. But I want to discuss it here.

I don't know the details of how her parents treated her, but I imagine they weren't great. They probably weren't even good. But I asked her if her parents influenced how she parented, and she said she's a better parent today because of how her parents treated her back then.

Most of us, if we had to choose between going through the hell we have gone through or having our children go through it, we would absolutely choose it all over again. And there are things we *must* go through ourselves to keep our kids from going through it. There are also things our kids *must* go through to navigate their lives. Through our parenting, mistakes and all, our children learn the resilience they need to become stronger and better, both as people and as parents. You did to!

If this is a concept that resonates with you, great. I am glad. If it's not, feel free to disregard it. I want you to know you are and always remain a choice. In the past, when I read books that initially triggered me, I would put them down for a while. When I returned to them, they usually offered me a profound breakthrough, and often, the breakthrough would be around the trigger. I know for some people, even the very word trigger can be a trigger.

If you find yourself triggered by anything said in this book, please know you do not have to agree with everything I say to find value in the book. I encourage you to do what you need to do to push through the trigger and see if something illuminates for you. And if it doesn't, you're welcome to schedule a free coaching session, and we can discuss the trigger.

I saw a social media post that said, "When the wound is ready to heal, the trigger will appear." I believe this to be true every single time. But triggers don't heal on their own. They have to be addressed. Looking at them can be uncomfortable, and that's why we stay stuck. But healing your triggers *is* the **best** thing you can do for your children.

Understand that each child is different.

Understanding isn't something we do well in the world today. We listen to argue or respond but don't listen to understand. As a mother, understanding our children is a skill we need more than others because we have precious babies to look after.

The second thing we must understand is that each child (of ours and in general) is unique and should be treated differently. As a mother of one son, I don't have firsthand knowledge of how to raise more than one, but I have five siblings (three boys and three girls), and in some ways, we were treated differently, and in others, we were treated the same and shouldn't have been.

An example from my perspective is my older sister and me. She was eight years older, and when she was sixteen-ish, she got a phone in her room. As sixteen-year-old girls do, she talked on the phone all the time and before call-waiting, this posed a problem for the household. When I was sixteen (and she was married with kids), my dad did not allow me to have a phone in my room because of the problem it caused eight years earlier.

When we treat every child the same, not only do they pay for crimes they never committed, but we miss the beauty of their individuality. The lesson I learned from that situation was that who I am does not matter, and I pay for the crimes of others. Those lessons turned into limiting beliefs which led me not to try because what's the point?

It is incredibly valuable to talk to our kids about why we do the things we do. Children *love* to ask why and believe me when I say a three-year-old is *not* asking why a thousand times because they want to annoy you. An eight-year-old is not asking you why to be disrespectful (It might start in the teen years, but I'll let you know when I get there!).

From the moment they are born, children try to figure out this crazy thing called life. They ask why because they are trying to understand. Period. They know you are their guide and protector. They want to know what you know and what you do not. One of the most Earth-shattering statements my mentor coach ever told me was the fact that my then six-year-old was still asking me why means I have not shut him down yet. The unfortunate truth is that so many of us are programmed out of asking why. If this is something we can intentionally unlearn and reprogram for ourselves, this can assist us in figuring out what bothers us and why. This will help us not only have a better connection with our kids but also with ourselves.

A wonderful thing to do when treating your children differently is to explain it to them. If one kid gets to stay up until 8:00 PM and another goes to bed at 7:30 PM, it is critical to clarify that a ten-year-old body does not need the same amount of sleep as a seven-year-old body. When we do not explain these things, they can make their own reasons why their brother gets to stay up later than them, and their own reasons are not usually empowering.

Recently, one of Zander's teachers had a strong reaction to Zander asking why. This was the first time he experienced a negative reaction to his inquisitive nature. I let him know the unfortunate truth: some teachers don't like the question why and he won't know who those teachers are until he asks the question. Explaining this to him hopefully helped Zander understand that his teacher's reaction had little to do with him.

Treating your children how they need to be treated means you need to know them. And there are few greater blessings in life than *knowing* your children.

The biggest way you should treat them differently is how you love them. You might be thinking, "Has she lost her damn mind? How on Earth is it a good idea to *love* my children differently? I love them the same!"

But they are not the same. None of us are the same. We all experience love differently. Loving your children equally is different than loving them the same. My most memorable moment with my son was when I asked him his love language. When he told me he feels the most loved when I snuggle him and I realized that was the thing I was doing the least, I was glad I asked the question. Much of my healing came from that question, and I wrote about it on a blog hosted on my website. Links to resources like this are in the back of the book.

Understand that we have good and bad days.

The third thing to understand is that we will have good and bad days. We all know that every day of our lives will not be a good day. I don't think growth would be possible if every day were a good day. We grow through our pain and typically label painful days as "bad days."

As humans, we label everything. It is a function of our brain to conserve energy. I invite you to start looking for the growth meant for you in the "bad days" and teach your kids to label them as growth days.

A personal example of this came in 2020. I had been getting up at 5:00 AM for a while, and one week, I had a particularly long week, although one could argue 2020 was a year of long weeks. One morning when my alarm went off at 5:00, I got out of bed, opened the bedroom door, and saw the cats sitting there, waiting for me to feed them. Every fiber of my being screamed, "NOPE!"

I went back to bed. Sorry kitties, I just couldn't.

But I also could not go back to sleep. I started thinking about how tired I was. Mostly physical, but some of it was emotional fatigue. In that moment, I was tired of being tired, and more sleep was not fixing the problem (I have been taking naps, going to bed earlier, and sometimes sleeping in).

I asked myself a powerful question. "How much longer am I going to choose to be tired of being tired?"

Yes, it's a *choice*.

I know my physical exhaustion had a large part (if not everything) to do with how physically inactive I am. I sit at my desk for most of my work, and all my hobbies are sedentary as well. When I go to the beach with my family, I need a recovery day because every muscle in my legs hurts from all the walking.

Enough was enough.

I got up out of bed, fed the cats, and went for a walk. The health app on my phone had been bugging me about walking 6000 steps a day (one hour of walking), and I just couldn't bring myself to silence it. I'd been silencing my body from talking to me for too long!

I walked for thirty minutes. While walking, I sent a Facebook message to my new coach friends and asked them to keep me accountable. It's much easier to stay in bed without accountability to someone who holds me to my commitments.

I started consistently reaching my 6000 steps. After a week of consistently reaching 6000, I increased by 500 until I got to 8000. I've adjusted my goal several times since mid-2020. My current routine consists less of getting steps and more about asking my body what it needs. Sometimes the dogs get involved in determining "what my body needs," but I make sure to reflect and ask.

It's been a process, and it's evolved.

I encourage you to start paying attention to your language. When you or your kids say it was a difficult day, ask yourself and/or them, "What lessons were meant for me today?" When you begin asking the question regularly, you naturally start labeling bad days as lesson days. I don't know about you, but I welcome a lesson day much more than I welcome a bad one. And I've found I don't have bad days anymore. I have moments that produce learning, and I feel better when I find the lesson. Try it. I dare you.

Integrity with boundaries.

The first step to integrity is learning how to set boundaries. We all have boundaries, whether we are aware of them or not. Most people I've encountered don't know how to communicate their boundaries clearly. I knew I didn't before I learned how!

In the last few years, I've noticed that the collective "we" of the world has a communication problem. A friend and I discussed this a few weeks ago because my son, Zander, asked me to define naïve. I know the word and how to use it in a sentence, but I didn't know how to define it for him.

Another example of this is the word feminism. Before I heard its definition, I would have gone to my grave, swearing I was not a feminist. But when it's defined as a person who believes women should be equal to men, then yeah, I'm a feminist. And to me, equal does not mean the same. I spoke of this in my blog, Understand.

How do we all have such different definitions of a word? Because we aren't taught our first language through definitions. We are taught by hearing our parents speak and then imitating them. Most of the time, we decide what a word means based on the context of a sentence. But Zander loves to ask, "Why?" and "What does that mean?" (Side note: We must nurture our children's creativity! It's such a beautiful thing to hold on to.)

When I first learned about setting boundaries through my coach, his example was making phone calls for your business. If you don't have a business, pick an area of your life you need to set a boundary and put that in the context of my example. If you need help, please contact me using the resources section at the back of the book.

If I say to my family, "I am making phone calls now," you might think you've set a boundary. When your husband or child interrupts you while making a phone call, you get angry that they aren't respecting your boundaries.

A perfect example of this was when I was recording a podcast, and Larry came home shortly after I hit the record button. I asked them to please quiet down. The noise only got louder. I did not realize Larry was trying to quiet Zander and the dogs. To me, in that moment, it meant Larry did not respect me or my job, and I got upset. After calming down, we discussed what I would like to happen while I am recording a podcast. During that conversation, it turned out that he did not know what I expected him to do while I was recording, he never knew *when* I was recording! We now have much clearer boundaries around when I'm recording a podcast.

If you say to your partner and/or your kids, "I am making phone calls from 7:00 PM to 8:00 PM, please do not interrupt me unless there's an emergency," that is a clear boundary, but you can be even more precise. Define what "an emergency" means and give an example. Needing a glass of water is not an "emergency."

After setting the boundary, you should ask for a receipt. What was your request? Do they agree to it? If they don't agree or they misheard your request, discuss it. Typically, you will not have to do this every time. Once the boundary is defined clearly and you get a receipt from your partner and/or kids, you should be able to say, "I am making calls from 7:00 PM to 8:00 PM. Please do not interrupt unless it's an emergency."

I once set a boundary with Zander. I told him I needed a break. I had been running like crazy for three solid weeks and hadn't taken time to unwind. In fact, I was **too tired** to do the thing I love to do to unwind! I told Zander I needed a day off, and the only thing I was going to do for him was give him snuggles and food. When he forgot later in the day and tried to have a tickle fight with me, I reminded him I was not doing tickle fights today, only snuggles. The next day, I felt ***much better!***

Integrity in your choices.

Integrity as a person is valuable for self-esteem and our self-worth. Integrity as a mom is key because our kids watch the show, not listen to the lecture. How frustrating was it as a kid to hear an adult say, "Do as I say, not as I do"? And how well did you listen to that?

I have compromised my integrity in several ways: Giving in to avoid dealing with the fight and saying yes when I mean no, and saying no when I mean yes. I will talk about the latter in the following tool.

Giving in. Sometimes we have to for our own sanity. It's a problem when it becomes a pattern or our default.

When I separated from my son's father, I struggled with depression. I was up to my eyeballs with responsibility and had no desire to take on more.

I never enjoyed cooking, but I just never took the time to figure out what to make. I have never been that person who lives to eat. I only thought about food when I was hungry. By then, I wasn't going to wait 30 minutes to an hour for my food to finish cooking. I ate *a ton* of instant food like macaroni and cheese and fish sticks. Pasta was one thing I made that felt like "I cooked."

They are watching the show.

During Zander's life, when kids are more willing to eat whatever is put in front of them, I gave him frozen hot dogs, chicken nuggets, and occasionally spaghetti (but that created too much work for me during that time, which made it super rare).

When I tried to give him something new, he pitched a fit and would not eat it. At the time, I was committed to peace between us and to him actually eating. I didn't like the idea of forcing him to sit at the table until he finished his food.

As he got older, friends and family noticed he wouldn't eat things unless they came in a box. By then, I was ready to introduce new foods to him. That was always part of my plan. I figured I could get him to try to eat new things when I could reason with him. Reasoning with a two or three-year-old is an exercise in misery, but an eight-year-old can understand that you need to eat nutritious food to grow up healthy.

My naive and ***passive*** plan backfired. The fight I was trying to avoid when he was younger found me when he was older. And it isn't any easier.

I forgive myself for the choices I made back then. I know I was doing the best job I could do at the time. If you are in a situation where you are up to your eyeballs in responsibility and you can't take on anymore, give yourself the grace to be where you are. Your kids will survive. I would also encourage you to seek support. You don't have to do it alone. It's okay to ask for help.

Integrity with your yes and no.

When I first started thinking of how mom guilt negatively affects us and our children's lives, compromising my integrity was the first thing that came to mind. I kept thinking about the times in Zander's life when I said "yes" when I wanted to say "no" and "no" when I wanted to say "yes." Most of the time, it happened because I felt guilty giving the answer I wanted or because I didn't want to deal with the fight.

As a parent, if we give in to our children for either of those reasons, we rob them of the lessons they need to learn. I genuinely believe that children can pick up on the energy we have when we say "yes" or "no" while out of integrity, and they will either imitate the behavior, exploit it, or both.

As an adult, when I went shopping with my mom, if I ever told her I liked an article of clothing, she would buy it. She would insist even if I told her she didn't have to. I always thought this was odd, and now I understand why she was doing that. While we were growing up, she didn't always have the money she wanted to spend on her kids. As an adult, she's doing it to make up for lost time.

There have been times in my life that I've done the same thing with Zander. If I told him no because I didn't have the money, I would "make up for it" by buying him things I didn't want to buy because he asked when I had the money. I wrestled with this throughout his life because I didn't want to teach him to have a lack mentality. I also didn't want him to think I only bought him things when he was "being good." I struggled with what I wanted to teach him because I have my own limiting beliefs around money and around performance that I didn't want to pass on to him, but since I still struggled with them, I didn't know how to teach him anything else.

Something that helped me with this was to take the time to explain to him why I was saying no. He would usually ask me why when I said no, which allowed me an opportunity to explain. It gave me a chance to tell him my reasoning for saying no instead of letting him come up with his own reasons. We, as humans, tend to make up disempowering explanations for things, and those turn into our limiting beliefs.

One of the examples I give later in the book is about a mom who chooses to go to the fair instead of paying her rent. It's difficult for me to believe she made a decision for any reason other than feeling guilty about telling her kids she didn't have the money to take them to the Fair. If she were my client, I would have encouraged her to tell her kids that keeping a roof over their heads is more important than going to the Fair. Children do understand when we take the time to explain.

We tend to feel guilty when we say "no" to our kids when we are saying "no" to something we actually wanted as a child. The truth is, there are lessons we learn through hearing "no," and when we say "yes," when we know we shouldn't, we rob our children of the lessons they need to learn. It's also essential to heal your relationship with the past when it comes to the things you wanted that you didn't get. What lessons were you meant to learn from that situation? Often, when we identify the lessons meant for us to learn, we can heal from the past to keep it from controlling our future.

As I wrote this, my friend, Tessa, said, "No is just a word, not a life story, life sentence, or form of punishment. Yes, is just a word as well."

One tool I teach clients is saying yes as no. The example we use is when your child asks for ice cream for breakfast. When I first heard this example, my embodied response was "Of course the answer to that is no!'

But my response was, "Yes, you can absolutely have ice cream after dinner this evening."

Another thing to be cognizant of when using the word "no" and sticking to it is that we want our children to also use the word no and stick to it. When your child is at a party and is offered drugs, what would you like their answer to be? And if their answer is no, would you like them to stand firm in that no or be talked into changing their mind?

Remember, they are watching the show, now listening to the lecture.

Love yourself.

If someone had told me ten years ago that one day I would write about how to love yourself, I would have laughed at them. I do not think I was aware of how I truly felt about myself, but I definitely didn't act like someone who truly loved myself.

But over the last three years, I have felt a difference in how I feel about myself. This makes me excited for my future as well as my son's. The premise of my podcast, *Imperfect Mommying: Better Parenting through Self-Healing*, is that our children are watching the show but not listening to the lecture. When I think about Zander growing up and knowing what it means to absolutely love yourself, it makes me excited for him.

You might wonder what loving yourself has to do with guilt. When you feel guilty about something you've done in the past, you're punishing yourself, and inside of that punishment, self-love can't exist. I heard someone say that you cannot be hateful and grateful at the same time. Those two emotions *cannot* exist at the same time. I believe the same is true about guilt and self-love. They can't co-exist because they are opposites of each other.

I got some inspiration from a self-love article at thelawofattraction. com. Their list has 15 ways to love yourself, and I'll address a few of them here.

Forgive yourself for your mistakes.

Forgiving yourself is ultimately what letting go of guilt is all about. When you do something in your life you wish you hadn't, or vice versa, you are looking back on the past with your current awareness and judging yourself for not making a better decision. But I don't think anyone ever thinks in the moment, "This is the worst possible decision I could make, but I'm going to do it anyway." Forgive yourself for not knowing better at that time. Understand that if it were supposed to be different, it would have been. Know that if we judge ourselves by the decisions we've made, we romanticize what could have been. However, when in reality, things could have been worse with a different decision.

Give yourself a break.

The month of August is a complete blur for me. I had a week of training, a week of implementing what I'd learned in training, a week I decided I needed to push myself harder because I was feeling so tired, and a week I took a break. You see, I needed to take a break after the week I was in training. Maybe for just a day or two. But I was excited about my training and immediately went into action. Looking back, I can also tell I was tired. The week I took off to recuperate turned into three because it was hard to regain momentum. If you can find a way to schedule yourself a break, you won't get burned out like I did, and you'll accomplish more in the long run.

Taking a break from your kids is equally important. When we become moms, we often forget that we are still humans with interests and desires of our own. We become wrapped up in our children and sometimes forget who we are. Not only is it healthy for you to have a break from them, but it's also healthy for them to be around other people too.

Make a list of your accomplishments.

This is an important one to me because I frequently forget all that I do. A friend always tells me she doesn't know how I do it all. Most of the time, I have no idea what she's referring to because I don't give myself credit for what I do. Making a list of accomplishments helps you acknowledge what you've done in your life. It enables you to pat yourself on the back and tell yourself you did an excellent job.

I took my own advice as I approached my 40th birthday. Since my friend Chellie passed away, I'd dreaded turning 40. She died suddenly two months before her 45th birthday, and it set in that we are not promised tomorrow. I felt the pressure that I wasn't doing enough to make my mark in the world.

Because I felt I hadn't accomplished enough in my 40 years, I sat down and wrote 40 things I had accomplished. Your list doesn't have to be the same as mine, but if you're a mom, you do a lot in a day, and we don't give ourselves enough praise for all we do. We are too busy comparing ourselves to the things other people do more of or better.

Love your child where they are.

What exactly does that mean?

When I wrote down *love your child where they are* as a third bullet point, and even when I first sat down to write this tool, I didn't know what it honestly meant. But after reading one of the best parenting books I've ever read, No-Drama Discipline by Daniel J. Siegel, M.D. and Tina Payne Bryson, Ph.D., I now have a better understanding.

If you're like me, you don't feel guilty for the moments when you have meaningful conversations or well-thought-out life lessons with your children. We create guilt in the moments when our kids are grating on our very last nerve, and we finally lose it.

One thing I learned in No-Drama Discipline is that discipline is used for teaching, not punishing. It's a different concept from what I've always thought of as discipline, but I'm drawn to the theory. Because as an adult who has multiple businesses, the first hurdle I had to cross was learning to detach between the connection between discipline and punishment. I know I'm not the only one who struggles with that.

Our energy shifts when we start looking at our children breaking rules and emotional instability as evidence of things we still need to teach them instead of behaviors that need to be punished. Ultimately, we can be more effective parents.

Another concept I loved from No-Drama Discipline is Connect and Redirect. When my son was having a meltdown over how difficult his math homework was, my first reaction was to get frustrated with myself, tell him to knock it off, and just focus (I know, I know, mother of the year over here).

Connect and redirect have offered me another approach. For starters, I stay calmer. Getting upset myself doesn't help him or me in the situation. If I can, I will put a hand on him and rub his leg, back or arm, as I know this helps him calm down. In extreme cases, I might pick him up, put him on my lap and rock him. Other times, I connect through words. In my opinion, the two most underutilized words in the English language are "I understand."

Once he's calmer, I will attempt redirection. Sometimes we need to take a break from math (although sometimes I wonder if his goal is to drive me crazy until I get fed up and let him out of the assignment). My son is reward oriented, and it's not out of the realm of possibility to offer him an extra five minutes of iPad time if he finishes the homework in ten minutes or less.

Connecting with others is something I absolutely love to do. This book helped shift my perspective on my goal as a parent. If discipline is something you struggle with, I highly recommend this book.

Trust your intuition.

In full transparency, trust is something I've struggled with. Trusting myself and trusting others. Sometimes even trusting my son.

As a mom, we aren't given a handbook to accompany our new baby, but we are given something that many women have stopped paying attention to—intuition. It's one of those things people ignore because maybe they don't understand or believe it's real.

I was never a mom who read all the parenting books. Zander was six years old when I read No-Drama Discipline by Dr. Tina Bryson and Dr. Daniel Siegel. I chose that book because I was having drama discipline at the time, and Larry said, "You do all this personal development stuff; why not pick up a parenting book?"

Leave it to me to find a parenting expert who disguises personal development with parenting advice. I became obsessed and bought all the books. Most of them remain unread at this point, but I have them!

When my son was born, I had an incredible support system. My mother-in-law stayed with me for a few days. After she left, my mom came, followed by my sister, who stayed with me for the six weeks my husband at the time was deployed. I was in a predominantly female direct sales company, and a large percentage of them were moms. I even had a friend that I referred to as "my friend who knows everything" because if I had a question about parenting (or anything else), she seemed to know the answer.

I am aware that not everyone has this type of support. I am also aware that not everyone hears the advice, "Take what resonates with you and discard the rest."

That was my parenting approach. I relied heavily on my intuition, although that's not what I called it then.

I remember there was a time right after my first surrogacy baby was born when my motherly intuition was too high to ignore. Zander was non-verbal at the time, but I knew everything he needed in a way I never did previously. I had just given birth but didn't have a new baby to care for. All the instinct transferred to him.

We all have that voice telling us to do this or do that, but how often do you listen to it?

There's no judgment in that question because if there were, I'd be a major hypocrite. I don't listen all the time, but most, if not all, of the time, I regret not listening.

Intuitive parenting takes time, but quieting your mind daily can help develop listening muscles. Some people call it meditation, but sometimes as my writing friend says, free writing can also help to clear cobwebs.

Reading books on parenting can be an effective way to increase your parenting knowledge. However, remember that parenting experts are just people with opinions who may have done more research than you. But research changes if you've followed health research on what is good and bad for you (think about all the times they've changed their minds about eggs). Why? Because everyone is unique. People are similar, but there are no two people alike. Even identical twins are different.

This is why parenting research should be taken with a grain of salt. Ask yourself, does this feel right? When I tried it, how did it feel doing it? How did my child react? Etc. Act, Assess, Adjust. If you try something that "fails miserably," tomorrow is a new day, and if your child is at an age where you can explain what you're doing, explain it. Ask for their feedback and take it with a grain of salt.

I can honestly say I've never regretted following my intuition. I have, however, regretted not listening to it.

Another way to develop trust with yourself is personal development.

I heard on a podcast once, "The better person I become, the better mom I become." It resonated so much that I named my podcast after it. If you are reading this book, you are committed to being the best mom you can be for your children. What better way to become a better mom than to get to know yourself and become a better person?

My personal development journey has been incredible. I've gone from never wanting to be alone because I was afraid of the things I would say to myself when I was, to truly enjoying every aspect of my life. Even doing the laundry! (Gasp)

Trust your children.

Trusting our children is one of the most valuable gifts we can give them.

When we are born, we know two things: love and desire. When a baby cries, it's because it needs something. Our babies don't try to manipulate us. All they know is that they get what they want when they cry.

Ultimately, manipulation is just a tool we humans use to get what we want. And somewhere along the line, we've labeled manipulation exclusively as bad. But I don't see it as black and white.

There's a concept I learned in No-Drama Discipline called Hearing Shark Music. You typically feel relaxed when you think of the ocean, see the waves rolling in, or hear calm and peaceful music playing. But when you look at the same image, and the theme music to Jaws is playing, you're no longer calm but probably feeling tense, waiting for a shark to attack.

When we hear "shark music" with our children and their behavior, we parents tend to take an innocent situation and turn it into something it is not. For example, Larry caught my son, Zander, up past his bedtime. Larry is convinced that because Zander admitted to sneaking around past his bedtime a million times, that was what was happening this time. When Larry sees Zander up past his bedtime, he hears shark music. And for good reason.

Even months after he was punished for the event, I believe Zander was telling the truth because of how adamantly he insisted that he was not sneaking around but investigating a noise. I have seen Zander try to lie about his actions, and frankly, he folds after some interrogation.

Trusting your child is vital to the bond you have with them. And trusting your intuition, plus checking to see if you're hearing shark music, will help guide you in situations where you don't know if you should trust them or not.

Trust your support team.

The African proverb is true: it takes a village to raise a child.

That proverb means that it takes a community of people to interact with a child for them to experience and grow up in a safe and healthy environment. I believe this to be true. Our children need to be exposed to several types of people in order for them to learn to deal with people who aren't like them.

The problem I see is that women often do not have a support group.

Later in the book, I talk about dealing with the death of my best friend last year. The connection I had with her rivals any other; I even considered her a second mother to Zander. Losing her was devastating to us both, and a year and a half later, I have friends I talk to, but nothing compares to that relationship.

We all need community. We all need a support system. But what is a support system? And what does it mean to trust your support system?

A support system can be anyone whose opinion you trust. It can be a friend, a family member, a teacher, or even an expert. It's okay to seek advice from others when faced with a new or uncertain situation. Trusting your intuition does not mean you cannot get input from others.

Along with trusting outside sources, it is fair to say you don't want to trust others blindly. That is where trusting yourself and your child comes in. You may get advice from a friend, family member, or expert you disagree with, which is okay. Not everyone will give you advice you agree with. But asking for help can help you feel like you are part of a community, giving you a jumping-off place, even if you do not take the advice.

I know from personal experience that people give unsolicited advice to moms, especially new moms. And depending on your relationship with them and your relationship with receiving advice, it can feel like a personal attack.

When receiving unsolicited advice, it is okay to ignore it. It is also okay to let them know you do not want it. I told loved ones that if I needed advice, I would be sure to ask. I thanked them for their suggestions and support but told them it was not necessary. I was fortunate enough to have people who listened to my requests.

Good Moms Don't Feel Disconnected from their Kids

*W*hen I was pregnant with Zander, I remember being incredibly excited. We tried for a year and a half before he was conceived. But, looking back, I never felt connected to him. The one exception was when I cried after hearing his heartbeat for the first time. For the most part, I went through the motions, doing all the things you're supposed to do as an expectant mother. I went to my prenatal appointments and tried to eat right, but the connection I saw in other moms during pregnancy was something I just didn't experience. When I went into preterm labor at 30 weeks, I imagined what my four-pound baby boy would look like. At that point, he became a real person to me. He became Zander.

For 14 months after he was born, my life felt picture-perfect. I had the family I desperately wanted, with a beautiful baby boy, a husband I adored, and I had pride in my position in the top 2% of my direct sales company. I had everything I wanted, but my foundation was built on a lie.

Zander's dad and I separated, and I fell into a deep depression. My whole life revolved around my family, and when it fell apart, I did too. I started to feel disconnected from Zander again because everything about him reminded me of his dad. All I wanted was to forget.

As time passed, I began to heal from my divorce, but the disconnection I felt from Zander continued. For years, I watched my best friend, Chellie, have this unbelievable bond with him. The way she connected with him was something I coveted. How did she do that? How were they this close? We discussed it several times. One time, I told her about my relationship with my dad. I was his only girl. My three brothers loved to watch and play sports with him, but I wasn't interested.

Looking back, I realized I tried connecting with him through my love languages of gift-giving and quality time. I'd go to the grocery store with him and ask him to buy me gum. But he just got irritated. I know my dad loved me and my brothers, but we all struggled to connect with him emotionally. He spent most of his time at work or with his nose in a book.

My connection with my mom always felt easy. She was a teacher and had four children at home, but I found a way to spend quality time with her. I followed her around the house while she did housework, and I talked her ear off about my day. Zander used to follow me around the house, too, until I asked him his love language. Once I started filling his "love bucket" the way that served him best, he no longer needed to seek it out by following me around.

Chellie said she didn't have anything in common with her dad either, but she started doing things he was interested in. She learned about cars and motors. She knew how to change the tires and the oil. This is a novel idea to me because, to this day, I have never even put air in my tires.

I tried to connect with my dad through sports. One time I tried out for the basketball team and didn't make it. But my half-hearted attempts weren't more than that. One of the reasons I started writing was to bond with my dad, but I never wrote anything he would be interested in.

Similarly, I have struggled to find common ground with Zander too. He has asked me to play Minecraft with him a dozen times before I finally broke down and did it. I do not think he's ever been happier. All he wants is to connect with me. I have never been a fan of video games. I like to play a few from the nineties, but that's about it. If my eleven-year-old could play video games all day, he would.

To find things we have in common, I have begun limiting his screen time to two hours daily. The first hour he gets outright, but he earns the other hour in 15-minute increments by doing something with or for me. Yesterday, he earned his extra hour by reading a book, taking a bath, doing homework, and riding his bike. I did these things with him. It was one of the most fun days we have had. He did not argue with me about doing his homework. He had fun going to the store. At the end of the day, he told me it was one of the best days ever. Now, we have a few things we enjoy doing together. I'm currently reading Harry Potter to him (he absolutely loved the movies), and we like to play Uno. He beats me most of the time, and he just loves throwing down the Draw Four card to make sure I have the most cards at the end.

I wasn't sure if any other mothers ever felt disconnected from their kids, but during one of the revisions of this book, my friend admitted she felt this way with her two girls when she was in "workaholic" mode. She would not have used that word to describe it, but she understood what I meant.

Maybe you feel detached from your children because you work out of the home and don't have the time with them you would like. The quality of time is typically more important than the quantity. If all you have with them is fifteen minutes before they leave for school or a half an hour before bed, make the time count. Come up with ways to make them feel special and loved, and it will leave a lasting impression on them.

The Truth

Good moms don't feel disconnected from their kids except when:

- *that's the model they grew up with.*
- *they are busy and overwhelmed.*
- *they are protecting themselves from getting hurt (more on that in another chapter).*

This isn't a complete list of exceptions to this rule. These were some I used to release my guilt. I've also worked on changing our relationship. If this is a rule you break, what is the exception that will free you? My examples may work for you, and they may not. Even if they do, spend some quiet time with yourself and create something that feels right to you.

Pro tip: If you struggle to find an exception (remember, there is one for every rule), take yourself out of the equation. What might cause another mom to feel disconnected from their kids? Sometimes this workaround allows you to find an exception that works for you.

Good Moms Don't Put Themselves First

When Zander was a little over a year old, I registered to attend a two-day conference approximately 45 minutes from my home. It was both fun and educational, and since my business began, I have never missed it. In fact, Zander was eight days old when I went the year before.

The plan for the weekend was that his dad, my husband at the time, would take care of him while I was gone. But when Zander got a fever, I got a call. "Come home," he insisted. "He wants his mom."

That night, I returned home to relieve my husband from sick-baby duty. I called my mom to ask for help because this event was important to my work, and I was also committed to helping one of the event speakers. She agreed to take him the next day, but when she picked him up, she said, "I thought the whole point of your business is 'God first, family second, career third.'"

Without a moment's hesitation, I responded, "Sometimes you have to put your career first to put your family first."

When you go to work, you put your family first. Without income, how can you pay for things? There seems to be an excessive amount of judgment about working moms. In a dual-income home or as a single mother (I've experienced both), what choice do I have? I was not born independently wealthy. And I know even if I were, I would be bored without a job to keep me busy. For about six weeks of my life, I had the ability to be a stay-at-home wife, and by the fifth week, I was searching for a job.

I have been blessed to be a work-from-home mom for most of my son's life. I began my home-based cosmetic business about a year before I got pregnant. Working from home also doesn't mean he has been with me 24/7. As nice as that sounds in theory, I would go crazy. Moms need breaks too. He did spend the first six weeks of his life with me at every single work appointment I had, and approximately fifty women held him during that time. I do not know if there is a correlation between that and how social he is now, but it played a part.

The Truth

Good moms don't put themselves first, except when:

- *putting their career first is putting their child first.*
- *putting themselves first is the best thing for their kids.*

Rachel Hollis is the author of Girl, Wash Your Face and Girl, Stop Apologizing. In her movie, "Made for More," she explains that women are like vases, constantly tipping themselves over for everyone else. They give and give until their vase is empty. We are nurturers by nature; of course, we want to take care of others. But when we are empty, what more do we have to give? When we put everyone's needs before our own – yes, even our kids – we will eventually run out of what's in the vase and then our kids, family, co-workers and even strangers get emptiness they don't deserve. When we fill our vase first, what happens when it becomes full? It overflows! That is why it is imperative to put our needs first. When our needs have been met, it is easier to meet the needs of others, and we will feel more fulfilled doing it. This is why self-care is vital and not selfish.

What does it look like to put your needs first? I can't answer that specifically for you, but it starts with spending time with yourself. Where you spend your time tells your subconscious what is important to you, therefore, spending time with yourself is an essential part of self-care.

For me, I wake up an hour earlier than the rest of my household, and I do what I want during the hour. A friend of mine stays up late for alone time because that's when she has the most energy. I used to avoid alone time, but as I've worked on myself over the past few years, I've learned to love it.

Another thing I do for self-care is connect with people. Connecting with others fills me up. I strive to reach out to someone every day, say hi, chat about their life and mine, and just be with people outside my home. I hear women tell me they don't have friends like they did before having kids. That's a warning sign to me because connection is such a huge part of life. You should connect with at least one person outside your significant other and your children.

I want to encourage you to find things that work for you and help feed your soul. Maybe try yoga or meditation. Those may be simple suggestions, but some things are cliché for a reason; they work!

We love our kids, and we put them first most of the time. Determining what revives your spirit can take effort, but it is worth the time it takes to figure it out. And then find the time to do it. One day, your kids, your relationships, and you will be thankful for it.

Good Moms Don't Ask for Help

Let's face it, women are expected to do it all: Have a career, keep the house clean, raise the kids, have a home-cooked dinner on the table, help with homework, head the PTA, bake 3,000 gluten-free, sugar-free chocolate brownies in four hours (because, of course, four hours is all the warning your child gives you despite knowing about the fundraiser since the first day of school...180 days ago). Never ask for help and do it with a smile on your face. I don't know about you, but I was never issued superpowers. To be honest, even if I could do it all, I don't think I would want to! I got tired just writing this paragraph, forget trying to accomplish all the things mommy culture expects of us.

In my home-based business, consultants, from the beginning, are encouraged to get help. As a business owner, your time is best used doing the high-dollar tasks and paying someone to do the things anyone can do or things you struggle to do. I've worked my business with and without an assistant. I am currently without because I have a program to help set my appointments, which frees up a significant amount of my time.

Every day I spend 15-30 minutes doing housework, an hour calling my customers, an hour writing, and the rest of the day varies with other tasks. Some days I'll spend more time calling customers, some days, I'll spend more time writing, etc. I do most of the day-to-day things around the house like dishes, laundry, and keeping things tidy, and Larry does the bigger jobs that don't need to be done daily. We have a good balance, and we set up our system by discussing what chores we like and dislike.

Over the past two years, I have worked with a personal coach. During that time, my coach asked me what is important to me. Side note: If you'd like, you can take a moment to do it now. It's better if you have someone ask you, "What's important to you?" over and over until you feel the list is complete. After you have a complete list of your priorities, rank the list. This is also best to do with a friend. They should ask, "What is more significant, A or B?" Do this for the full list, and you will have ranked your priorities.

I did this exercise three or four times before I understood why it was critical to know my priorities. My family is at the top of my list and having a clean home ranks in the top five. Larry hates doing laundry and dishes (most of us do), but when I discovered his top love language is acts of service, doing those chores stopped being such a pain in the butt. It became one of the ways I showed my love for him. I know if I hadn't made the connection between my chores and serving my family, eventually, I would have become resentful of being the only one taking care of the house.

The Truth

Good moms don't ask for help, except when:

- *you haven't been issued your superwoman powers.*
- *you need help.*

Do you feel like you are expected to do it all alone because you think a good mom should do it all on her own? Or because a good mom shouldn't need help? Feeling like you can't ask for help can be dangerous and can lead to resentment.

When I was first divorced from my son's dad, I resented the fact that he could just walk away, or move eight hours away, pretend he was no longer a dad if he wanted, and I was "stuck" with the kid. At the time, I had no help unless I paid for it, and I didn't have money to spare. I had family members judge me for the frustration I felt about having to do it alone. I felt helpless and incredibly unsupported.

A few months ago, I was traveling home from an event and started thinking about my current life. I became overwhelmed with gratitude for the support system I developed. Tears of joy and appreciation flowed down my cheeks as I texted three of my biggest supporters how grateful I was to have them in my life. In six years, I went from extreme depression and desperation to a moment of pure fulfillment because I got comfortable asking for the support I needed.

It's okay to take the S off your chest and the cape off your back. If you've spent your life believing you need to be a superwoman in order to be a good mom, you have permission to let that belief go. Ultimately, your children will remember your time together more than the dish-free kitchen counter or dust-free bookshelves.

I have some tricks I use to keep from getting overwhelmed. They are as follows:

- **I make a "Ta Da!" list.** A To Do list is never done. It's a list of things to...do... But making a list of the things you need to get done, and checking off things as you complete them gives you a sense of accomplishment (you can see the progress you've made, ta da!), you get to check off the boxes as you complete the tasks (so satisfying), and it keeps you focused on what you need to do next.

- **Kid Swap.** Ask a few friends if they would be willing to be a standby babysitter in case of emergency. For me, it helps knowing I have a backup if my regular sitter can't watch him. You could also offer to kid swap with your mom friends. I will watch yours one day, and you can watch mine another day. As a mom of an only child, Zander loves play dates. Check if your hometown has a babysitting co-op (apparently, it's a thing).

- **Get Help.** Outsource tasks you hate (house cleaner, yard work, grocery shopping, etc.). If that's not an option for you financially, maybe you and your partner can swap the chores. If that's not an option, try getting your kids involved. It's never too early to teach them responsibility.

- **Simplify Daily Tasks.** Meal prep is another way to minimize day-to-day chores. Make a larger meal on Sundays and Wednesdays and have leftovers a few days a week. Frozen meals also won't kill your children or your family. Neither will fast food now and again.

- **Do something special for yourself!** Personal care is NOT selfish! It is SELF-care! We need to take care of ourselves because most of the time, no one else is. Get a pedicure, have a girl's night out, take a nap, or take a shower (alone!).

If asking for help is not the good mom rule you are breaking, but you still feel like you should be doing it all alone, take some time to figure out where the guilt comes from. Maybe you watched your mom do it all on her own, and you think that's a requirement to be a good mom. Maybe you grew up doing it all on your own because no one took care of you. Take some time to pinpoint the cause of your specific guilt and what your exception to the rule is. This will be the difference between letting it go and staying stuck.

Good Moms Don't Work Outside of the Home

I didn't always know I wanted to be a mom, but I knew if I was going to have kids, I wanted to be able to stay at home with them. My recruiter in my home-based business was a work-from-home mom, and her lifestyle was something I wanted once I knew it could be done. Plus, growing up, I watched my mom work as a teacher, then come home and work some more around the house. It looked exhausting.

For years I talked about wanting to be a stay-at-home mom when I introduced myself at my skincare classes. The whole truth was that I didn't want to be a mom for about a decade or more. I spent the summer before my senior year as a camp counselor coupled with years of babysitting, I was burned out on kids. Then my biological clock kicked in, and I decided I wanted a baby. At that point, I never thought about the kind of mom I wanted to be. I was a work-from-home mom because I became an Independent Beauty Consultant with one of the top direct sales companies about a year before he was conceived. It wasn't until I was going through a divorce that I decided staying at home with him was extremely important to me.

I mentioned earlier that I was a surrogate. While going through my divorce, I found an ad on Craigslist looking for women to help families grow. I was looking for a way to keep my work-from-home status, but I also needed financial security. Being a surrogate was always something I wanted to do, and I felt lucky to have the opportunity.

While writing this chapter, I asked a group of women if they felt guilty about working outside the home. I interviewed a single mom who worked seven days a week to support herself and her kids. She felt guilty about working as much as she did, especially because her daughter had ADHD. The symptoms were worse while Mom was out of the house working. Once she became a stay-at-home mom, her daughter's behavior improved dramatically.

It's difficult when you feel like the thing you have to do to survive and support your children financially is something that hurts your children emotionally. But sometimes life throws you curve balls, and you do things you never dreamed of to take care of your little ones.

This mom did what she had to do (working seven days a week) to provide for her children. She changed her life, and now she's at home with her kids. There's no shame in doing what you must do until you can make changes.

The Truth

Good moms don't work outside of the home, except when:

- *they want or need to work outside of the home.*

Many moms don't have the option to stay at home. Some moms wouldn't want to stay home even if it was an option. Since some women have a choice one way or another, there's shaming from both sides. How could you want to leave your kids to go to work? Why would you want to pay someone else to raise your kids? Do you stay at home with the kids? What do you do all day? Are you too lazy to get a real job?

The truth is that a good mom is a fulfilled woman and if you are content being home with your children, then do it. If you have a passion outside of the home, you are not paying someone else to raise your children. You are raising your children, and someone else is loving them while you are fulfilling your passion. If you're a working mom who wishes they were home with their kids, but your financial situation doesn't allow you to be home, your kids know how and what you provide them.

Feeling guilty about where you are in your life, wherever that is, will not change your situation. If you don't like where you are, then make changes. I know some women feel stuck. That's how I felt: alone, helpless, unsupported. Through the small shifts I made, everything changed.

Minor changes can be easy to make. In some situations, the only change possible is a shift in the way you think. We can change the way we perceive things if we set the intention to do it. An example of a mind shift is what I mentioned in the last chapter about doing laundry and dishes. When I found out Larry's love language was acts of service, I stopped thinking of laundry as a terrible, endless chore I must do. I started thinking of it as an act of loving him. Since then, there have been days I've actually been sad I didn't have any laundry to do.

Another example of a small shift that anyone can do is focus on gratitude. Even if you're unhappy with everything in your life, there's something someone wants. Wake up every day and decide, "This is going to be a great day." Then create a list of three things you are grateful for every day and send it to a friend or post it on social media. I learned this from a book called "Thank and Grow Rich." Trust me. It works.

A mom I interviewed complained about her husband and mom not giving her the hour of alone time she desperately needed for her personal care and sanity. I suggested that perhaps she could leave her daughter at daycare for an extra hour. She didn't like the idea, but she became forceful with taking alone time. The next time we talked, she had a much calmer presence about her. Things aren't perfect in her life, but it's a start.

Can you think of a small shift you can make to improve your happiness and fulfillment in your life? If you are struggling to find your shift, these are the types of things a life coach like me can help you with.

Good Moms Don't Let Their Kids Eat Frozen Food

(and they don't let their kids become picky eaters)

$\mathcal{O}$ ne morning while writing this book, I woke up at 4:30 AM to a podcast Larry had on as background noise. I don't recall what they were talking about before I heard one of the men say, "Fish sticks are the perfect meal for lazy moms." I couldn't go back to sleep after. My blood boiled.

For most of my life, I couldn't have cared less about cooking. I never thought about food until I was hungry. By then, the last thing I wanted to do was prepare food and wait an hour to eat it. In high school, the only thing I made regularly was Mac and Cheese and white rice. As a young adult, those individual Mac and Cheese cups were a staple in my home.

My husband attended culinary school, and I was lucky because he loved to cook. When I cooked, it was always pasta. I loved breastfeeding Zander because I didn't have to think about what to feed him. When he started eating solids, jars of baby food were super simple. And later, when I did start cooking, we ate pasta frequently.

When my son's dad and I divorced, I suffered a severe depression. During that time, Zander started exhibiting signs that he was on the autism spectrum. It was a major struggle to deal with his emotional breakdowns when I barely held myself together. There were times I wanted to throw myself on the ground and cry too!

He was evaluated for a year and a half and was ultimately diagnosed with having characteristics of an autistic spectrum disorder. I could only focus on getting the two of us through it alive. I had moments when I wanted to give up on life and other moments I wanted to give up on being a mom. At the time, the last thing I could think about was learning to cook well-balanced meals.

Zander is also a super picky eater, which is common for children on the spectrum. My son's diet was chicken nuggets, corn dogs, and anything with marinara sauce. There were only a few other things I could get him to eat. The handful of times I tricked him into eating fish sticks (disguised as "long chicken nuggets") was a win.

I've come a long way since then, and my son has too. I still struggle to get him to try new things. But as an eleven-year-old, I have explained to him the importance of having variety in his diet. For me, a big win is that he loves most fruits and even a few vegetables.

The Truth

Good moms don't let their kids eat frozen food, except when:

- *you feel you are at capacity with the things you are dealing with in your life.*
- *it's the only option because of time constraints.*

Good moms don't let their kids become picky eaters, except when:

- *they are picky eaters (i.e. we don't let them become anything).*
- *it's the best you can do, and you don't want the fight.*

There is tons of pressure for moms to be perfect, do everything right, keep up with the house, the kids, relationships with family, friends, and significant others, and be the breadwinner in some cases. The problem is that moms are only human. We have good days, bad days, overwhelming days, exciting days, and depressing days. We go through everything everyone else does, and we also have younger humans to care for.

When I heard the guy on the podcast call "fish stick moms" lazy, it triggered my guilt. It also made me angry because I advocate for moms. I've been called lazy by people in my life because of the way I've let Zander eat, but I had to choose my battles. I know it's essential for kids to eat healthy, well-balanced meals. And some days, a well-balanced meal is a pipe dream. All I can say is, "Do the best you can, Mom." Every day is another opportunity to improve slightly from the day before.

The most important thing is to love yourself through the process.

Good Moms Don't Need Breaks from Their Kids

"*I*f you love your kids, you shouldn't want free time." I heard this from a few women during my interviews.

The thought hurts my heart because it's far from the truth. Yet many moms feel guilty for wanting time away from their children. Needing time alone or with friends or other adult humans doesn't mean you love your kids less. People have needs. Spawning a mini-you doesn't make those needs disappear. Nor does it make them or *you* less important.

Earlier, I mentioned there was a time I didn't want to be a mom anymore. On one particularly difficult day with Zander, my mentor, Mimi, listened to me as I sobbed. I don't remember specifically what was going on at that time, why I felt overwhelmed, or what prompted my outburst, but I let myself scream the words, "I don't want to be a mom anymore!"

Reflecting on that moment, I must have been hysterical. I had reached a breaking point, and for a few moments, I regretted my decision to become a mom. I don't think she knew what to say to me. I remember we hung up the phone, and after a while, she called me back. She told me she knew a woman willing to adopt my son, and if

I didn't want to be a mom anymore, I had options. I was at a loss for words, but then I realized I just needed a break.

Feeling overwhelmed by my situation and not understanding personal care (taking time to feed my mind and soul outside of being a mom) led to feeling unqualified. I wasn't getting time alone, nor was I getting the support I needed from myself or others. I felt like I couldn't do it anymore.

The Truth

Good moms don't need breaks from their children, except when:

- *they do!*

I spent a good part of my life afraid of being alone. My sister used to say I was like a mermaid because "I want to be where the people are." Being alone became a lot less scary when I started working on myself. And now I crave time to myself. I love waking up at 6:00 AM, having time to collect my thoughts, be with myself, and do what I want.

When I started giving myself the time I needed, I needed less. My alarm goes off at 5:55 AM every morning. Some days I hit snooze and go back to sleep. Other days, I wake up, go to the couch, and pass out again. Either way, I don't feel guilty because whatever I do, I know I need it that day.

There are days when Zander wakes up shortly after I do. Because I do my best to honor my needs, the times he wakes up early feel like bonus time with him. Before, I felt irritated if he woke up early.

Giving yourself the things you need will make you happier and more fulfilled. Your children will get much more from you than they will from an overworked, stressed-out, grumpy mom who never leaves.

Good Moms Don't Pursue Their Goals and Dreams

*N*ow that you're a mom, you're supposed to sacrifice your goals and dreams for your kids. How did that feel to read that statement? Did it feel like a fact? Did it feel like the biggest lie anyone could ever spout? Maybe a bit of both?

I was triggered when I heard a friend of mine say those words. Part of me wanted to scream, not at her, but at this lie she believed. Part of me wanted to cry because I knew she was not the only mom living this terrible lie. I might have been one of them a few years back.

In second grade, I wrote a story on a 5x7 Post-It note. It was about a young girl who ran away from home but returned when no one noticed she was missing after an hour (it was nonfiction). My mom saved it for fifteen years in my memorabilia book. When I found it, I realized I had always wanted to be a writer. At sixteen, I wrote a young adult romance. I posted it on the fan-fiction website I managed, and because of all the positive feedback I received, I knew I would publish it one day. By the time I was twenty-eight, I had turned it into a trilogy and self-published the first book.

Shortly after, I lost my job in Corporate America and started my own home-based business. A year and a half later, I gave birth to my son. Eleven years after that, this is the first novel I've finished in those thirteen years (and I have another one I'll be releasing shortly about my surrogacy journeys).

I gave up on my dream of being a writer. For many of those years, I used my business and being a mom as the reasons I no longer had time to write. The funny thing is, as I'm writing this book, I am still a mom and have all the same responsibilities in my business.

The truth was when I published my book nearly 12 years ago, I expected to be the next J.K. Rowling or Anne Rice; famous beyond my wildest dreams, living off my book sales, and writing full-time in exotic places around the world. When that didn't happen, I started questioning my writing and storytelling skills. I couldn't have been all that good because if I was, I would have sold more than 100 copies. Never mind the fact that, at the time, I knew nothing about self-promotion, networking, or sales.

That's the funny thing about the mind; its highest commitment is to our emotional and physical safety, not our happiness or aspirations. My unmet expectations became a limiting belief: I wasn't a good enough writer to make my dreams come true. To protect myself from getting hurt again, I subconsciously looked for things I could blame for not writing anymore. My son and my business became those reasons.

The Truth

Good moms don't pursue their goals and dreams except when:

- *they have goals and dreams they want to pursue and make time for them.*
- *they want to show their children how to work hard for what they want.*

If you think of your family as the thing that is stopping you from getting what you want, they are now your burden. Are your kids a burden in your life? Or are they the most amazing blessing you could have been given?

Maybe some women feel totally and completely fulfilled by being a mom. The sun rises and sets on their happy, healthy children, and they are fulfilling their aspirations by raising them. If that's you, I admire you. Being a mom isn't a job that should be taken lightly. You're responsible for another human life. It should be a top priority.

And if you have dreams for your life outside of being a mom, I am with you. My sister-in-law said it best. When she thought about her life, she asked herself, "Would I work even if all my financial needs were being met?" It was a resounding "yes." That could be how you know if you have another calling beyond being a mother.

Even if you're fulfilled by being a mother, it's also essential to have something in your life that you do for yourself. Someday your children will leave home, and if they were the only thing that filled your day, you are more likely to experience empty-nest syndrome. When you have interests and hobbies outside of the kids, the transition they make from your home won't feel traumatic.

Don't keep putting off your goals and dreams until the kids leave the house. You will find a way if you really want to do it. If you don't, you'll find an excuse. Saying you can't because of the kids is making them your burden.

If you make a decision, you can always change your mind. You can't go back to where you were before the decision, but you can make a new choice from the new place. If you decide not to pursue your dreams or wait until a better time, you can do that. Just don't look back twenty years from now and wish you had made a different choice. No amount of wishing will change the past.

Good Moms Don't Let Bad Things Happen to Their Kids

W hen Zander was four, my best friend, Chellie, and I decided to move from an apartment we shared into a house. The deadline to leave our apartment was upon us, and we were still short on funds to pay for the moving truck we needed. Chellie went to San Francisco to drive for Uber for three days. I wanted to help, but I needed someone to watch Zander. I went through my phone and found the number of a former sitter. She wasn't available, but her mom and 13-year-old sister were. And they were willing to watch him overnight.

I was ecstatic. I'd never driven for Uber in San Francisco before, and I kept hearing about how much money you could make in a short amount of time. *Spoiler alert: It wasn't what it was cracked up to be, but we were still able to come up with the money in time.*

After the move, I contacted this sitter a few more times, and her mom and sister were always available. One afternoon, I picked Zander up from school and told him we were going to her house. He began to protest. He told me he didn't want to go because they didn't have toys to play with. When that didn't work, he burst into tears and told me the real reason he didn't want to go. She had been inappropriate with him.

My heart stopped. A million thoughts raced through my mind. What the hell? She's 13 years old, how is this possible? Where was her mom? What the heck happened?!

That last question is one that still plagues me. To this day, I don't know exactly what happened with his sitter. I reported it to Child Protective Services first because a 13-year-old girl propositioning a small boy screamed abuse to me. I also filed a police report because something criminal had occurred, and I wanted justice!

Nothing ever came from my reports. The mom and 13-year-old denied anything happened, and Zander didn't want to talk about it for over a year. I respected his wishes. Occasionally, he would mention her name. He remembers the apartment they lived in; he sees it all over town (not the actual apartment, but he thinks he recognizes it). His story has changed some, and I still don't know the details. I can't decide if that's a good or a bad thing. The situation still makes me sick.

For years, I was haunted by my decision to leave him with her. As his primary caregiver and arguably the person who loves him the most in the world, it was and is my job to protect him. As far as I was concerned, I had failed.

I believed that good moms protect their children, and I let something happen to him. This guilt was sneaky, though. It wasn't until recently that I realized how much it affected me. I started to snap when anyone asked me questions about it. I got angry with the people I trusted to care for him if they did anything different than I expected. They became the enemy. The circle of people I could trust got smaller and smaller.

When I realized how bad I felt, I told my coach. We were headed to a week-long event, and I told her to keep me from chickening out on addressing it. She asked everyone in the room what they wanted to work on, and despite my desire to fix this issue, everyone's hand went up except for mine. We went around the room sharing the things we felt guilty about. After everyone spoke, I raised my hand and said, "I let my son get hurt."

I was guided through the guilt exercise I've used in this book. When it was over, I felt lighter, like a 40-ton sack of bricks had been lifted from my shoulders. I was smiling more, and within hours, I was clearer about my life purpose.

I want to help moms let go of their guilt.

Since then, my eyes have been opened to the freedom you can feel by letting go of the mom guilt. I've grown closer to Zander. And it's the catalyst for writing this book.

When I first wrote this chapter, I didn't want to give the details of his story. I kept thinking, "It's not my story to tell; it's his." My life coach asked me why. It was then that I realized I was still ashamed of what happened. I let go of the guilt at my retreat, and when I started thinking about sharing this story to help others, I picked up the shame. Ultimately, I didn't tell the details because I didn't know them. That is a whole other type of torture.

The Truth

Good moms don't let bad things happen to their kids, except when:

- *they make decisions based on the information they have at the time.*

It is part of our job as parents to protect our children, but sometimes things happen that are out of our control, and beating ourselves up for not knowing what the outcome might be doesn't change what happened.

It is our job to protect them and sometimes that protection happens after the fact in the form of being their voice when they can't speak for themselves. But when something happens to them that you didn't intend, holding on to the guilt for not knowing what you didn't know isn't fair to you and doesn't serve your children.

The Incident with Zander happened nearly four years ago, and for three years, I beat myself up for not knowing better. Subconsciously, I kept him at a distance because someday, I imagined he would resent me for not protecting him. I protected myself from his future rejection.

Since letting go of the guilt, I have a closer relationship with him. For the first time that I can remember, I felt a closeness to him that was missing. It was like when you have a plastic cover over a couch, you can't feel it.

If your son or daughter has gone through an experience that you feel you should have protected them from, forgive yourself for not knowing better. As always, do your best in the future.

In my life, and most recently as a Life Coach, I have heard stories of parents who swept this situation under the rug, made excuses for the abuser, or flat out didn't believe their child instead of getting help and/or justice for them. If a child tells you something has happened, believe them. Make a police report. Get counseling for *you and them*.

I couldn't imagine doing anything differently than what I did after the fact, but many people don't know what to do in that situation. If it weren't for my friend, Chellie, I wouldn't have known how to react either. My hope is that if you know better, you can do better. But more than anything, I hope you don't have to go through this with your kids.

Good Moms Don't Struggle

I interviewed my friend Samantha who felt guilty when she said "no" to things her kids wanted. Her family was on a super strict budget, down to the penny, and if what the kids wanted wasn't in the budget, the answer should have been no.

I had a temp job at an eviction law firm, and an attorney told me of a family that was being evicted. He asked the mom why she hadn't paid rent that month. Her response was, "The fair was in town." She let her family lose their home because she couldn't say "no" to her kids. I don't know if that mom was evicted, and I never spoke to her about her choices.

As a life coach, I believe deep down, both women have the same mom guilt, and they unintentionally teach their children about money. One mom shows her kids how to set and follow a budget. Although they may whine about not getting what they want in the moment, one day, they will look back. They will appreciate their parents for keeping a roof over their heads instead of giving in to their every whim. The other mom will show her kids too many negative examples about responsibility and priorities to list!

Kids want what they want, but it's our job, as parents, to say "no" sometimes. If you say "yes" to everything they want, the "yes" stops being special. Your children become entitled, and when you do start to say "no," they start to fight back. How often have you seen a kid at Walmart or Target meltdown because their caregiver said "no?"

One story comes to mind: I was with Zander after he came home from visiting his dad and grandparents for a week. He must have asked me for a toy fifty times that day, and I deliberately told him "no" because he needed a reminder of what the word meant. I reached my breaking point when he asked me to buy him a sponge because he was that desperate to hear a "yes." I sternly replied, "If you ask me for anything else, I will throw away your toys at home." A man in line ahead of me, turned to me with a disgusted look and in a judgmental tone, said, "Really?"

I've been through periods where he gets a toy every time we go to the store. Other times, I'm more selective about getting him something. I have had a spending problem in the past, and I have struggled when I have to say "no." I admire the mom with the budget because that area is not my strong suit.

The Truth

Good moms don't struggle, except when:

- *they have unmet expectations for their lives.*

If you struggle with guilt for telling your kids "no," ask yourself where the guilt comes from. What is the "good mom rule" you think you're breaking?

I mentioned earlier, one of my love languages was gift giving/receiving, and I would ask my dad to buy me gum at the store. That irritated him to no end because he didn't want to tell me "no," and he didn't want to spend the money. Something I've started doing with my son is explaining to him why I say "no" when I say it. Recently, I've been saying "no" to buying toys because he doesn't play with them unless he has friends over, which is seldom.

We love our kids, and we want the best for them. But humans learn more through adversity than they do when times are easy, especially tiny humans. Sometimes they learn better lessons from hearing the word "no" than from hearing 1,000 "yeses."

Saying no is also modeling no and like I mentioned in earlier chapters, our children are watching the show not listening to the lecture. There are so many moms who say yes when they want to say no, like baking cookies, and volunteering and doing for others at their own expense. This leads to burnout and resentment and moms who have so little left to give themselves and even their families. There are so many reasons saying no is truly an act of saying yes and teaching this to our kids is a necessary lesson for us all.

When we say "yes" to one thing, we are saying "no" to something else. In a previous chapter, I talked about making a list of what is important to you. You can use this list to guide you on what you say yes and no to.

Good Moms Don't Lose Their Cool with Their Kids

$\mathcal{R}$ecently, at my nephew's wedding, I had the opportunity to sit down and talk with my youngest brother. He is a teacher, basketball coach, and father of two cute little boys (I might be biased). My brother and I don't get much one-on-one time and during our conversation, he told me he admires my patience with my son. This isn't the first time he has commented on my patience with Zander. I believe the first time he said it was via text, and my heart broke. At the time I thought it was the furthest thing from the truth. If I got a nickel every time I lost my cool with my son, I would be sitting here, writing this book from the comfort of my very own private island.

I once saw an Armenian comedian who said Armenians are master negotiators. They are from a country surrounded by people who don't want them there, and they negotiate everything. "How about this? How about this? How about this?" My immediate thought was, "All children must be Armenian, then. Especially mine!" (He's actually 25%, but I made my point.) Zander is the master at it. He knows he's cute and how to use that to his advantage, and I know he is not the only one. It doesn't help that he used to say, "pweeese," and we encouraged it. Every parent has probably said their child could be a lawyer someday, and my son is no different. He could argue with anyone and hold his own.

Having a child that will keep asking until I finally give in, I've developed a few techniques to keep him from manipulating me into doing whatever he wants, whenever he wants. But let me tell you, learning to hold my ground when he tried to get his way was not easy, and I made a ton of mistakes along the way.

One time, when Zander was about 18 months old, he was doing something I can't remember now, and I spanked him. For the first 16 months of his life, I don't think I had done that at all, but it had become a habit by that point. From then on, when he did something I didn't like, he got swatted.

That day, after I had spanked him, and he didn't cry, I spanked him again. And again. And again. And then I stopped. Not because he started crying but because my hand started to hurt. I sat there in tears because I had let myself get to that point. I remember being spanked only two times in my life, once by each parent, and neither of them hit me hard enough that it hurt. And I wasn't spanking him to correct his behavior, at least not at the end I wasn't. I finally realized what I was doing: taking out my anger and frustration at where I was in my life on that sweet boy.

That was the last time I spanked him. I realized that I probably would have had to spank him hard enough to break my hand before he might show that he felt pain. And if that was the case, there had to be better ways of disciplining him.

The Truth

Good moms don't lose their cool with their kids, except when:

- *they are human (yes, the exception can be that simple).*
- *they are not putting self-care first.*

- *they are overtaxed emotionally.*
- *they use it as a catalyst for change.*

If spanking is your form of discipline, I invite you to check in with why you do it. Perhaps that is how you were raised, and you are repeating history. But spanking should never be done out of anger. In fact, even though I was spanked as a child and that is what was modeled for me, I now believe that spanking should not be done at all. I have learned far better ways of teaching and redirecting our kids than ever having to resort to spanking or even being punitive. The solution seems counterintuitive, however connecting before correcting and redirecting is exponentially more effective on multiple levels. In addition to teaching our children, we keep the connection we have with them strong and healthy.

Every child is different and has unique needs when learning how to behave. Discipline is something that should correct a behavior, and somewhere along the way, spanking became the one-size-fits-all solution.

I felt guilty about how I behaved when Zander was younger. Years after I had stopped spanking my son, when I got angry, my son was afraid of me, and it hurt my heart. I asked my life coach how I could help him know I was safe, and his response was, "Be safe."

I have made significant changes in how I relate to him. I talk to him when I lose my temper and explain that it isn't about him. I am still human, and reacting with anger toward a situation is still a struggle of mine. But I am proud of the fact that I have filled my parenting toolbox with substitutes for spanking and while I am not perfect, I stay focused on the progress I've made and continue to make.

If this is something you struggle with and would like to change, there are countless books and parenting programs that can guide you through those changes. Parent Education is part of the foundation of what my friend Melanie Soloway does. Find a teacher you resonate with and use them to *guide* you along your journey.

Realizing this is an issue for you is the first step to change, but it's just the first step. Other steps follow. Some things I've done:

- **Self-care.** I know I may sound like a broken record, but this is a huge part of the changes I've made. Ensuring my needs are met goes a long way toward not taking my day out with the people I love.

- **Forgive yourself.** You are not perfect and never will be. Neither am I. We all make mistakes. We can't change the past; all we can do is learn from it.

- **Total Truth Letter.** In the next chapter, I will explain what this is but it's something that can help. When we lose our cool, it's not our situation that makes us explode. The problem might be that final drop in the bucket that causes the water to overflow. Keeping our emotions locked inside makes us a ticking time bomb.

- **Ask for support.** If you don't want to go to a therapist, or even a life coach (which I recommend because you can get an action plan tailored to you), then ask a friend. We tend to think we are the only person that struggles with our situation. You're not. Talk to a friend. Take a class. Join a parenting community. I have created one on Facebook, called The Imperfect Mom Community and I would love to see you there. If you choose not to join my group, do a Google search. Do something that will guide you to healing and moving on.

Good Moms Don't Leave The Father of Their Kids

Zander's dad and I were only married a few months before we started trying for a baby. However, we didn't get pregnant for over a year and a half. We had decided to choose to be happy together with or without a baby, and whatever was meant to be would be. I had completely put having a baby out of my mind when I took a pregnancy test, which was positive.

We didn't have a perfect marriage by any means, but I remember being happy. I had the family we tried for, and everything felt perfect. And then it wasn't. Our relationship ended around the time Zander was six months old, and I suffered from postpartum depression. But I didn't know it was over until approximately eight months later. I'd had enough, and I left.

My guilt as a mom settled in after I left his dad. I didn't want Zander to grow up like I did: split between two homes, having step-parents and step-siblings. I am grateful for those same stepparents, step-siblings, and half-siblings now, but when you're a kid, all you want is your mom and dad together. I didn't want to repeat the divorce cycle with him, and I didn't want him to be the third-generation son raised with dad outside of the home.

At first, when he asked why we split up, we both told him that we stopped getting along. I'm pretty sure Zander thinks if his dad and I get within a mile of one another, we will spontaneously start arguing. The second part of the explanation was that we didn't want him to grow up in a family with arguing parents. I stopped saying that because it was untrue, and I felt it was blaming him for the divorce. We don't tell him the whole story because I don't believe in parent bashing to the child, especially in a father/son relationship. But I wanted to add to my explanation. I told him that I wasn't happy back then. We couldn't stop fighting; instead, we stopped talking, and when I no longer had that connection to him, I was miserable. Without both partners willing to make a change, I didn't feel I had any other options at the time.

The Truth

Good moms stay with the father of their kids, except when:

- *they can be a better person and set a better example by separating.*

I met a mom after writing my book who finally left the father of her children, but not soon enough. Her daughter remembers the abuse, and now she feels guilty for not leaving sooner. If you are staying in a toxic relationship for the kids, please don't.

You have two options right now. 1) Work on the relationship and/ or yourself to find a way back to being in love with your spouse. A book I've used that has helped me in my current relationship is called "Getting the Love You Want" by Harville Hendrix and Helen LaKelly Hunt. He actually suggested I read it before we were ever officially dating, and it's what's given us such an incredible foundation. If you feel your relationship is salvageable, read this book and implement their teachings. I believe with all my heart that it's worth a try. And if that's not an option, 2) leave. Staying "for the kids" is not what's best for them. Seeing their parents happy and in a healthy relationship is.

If you and their dad can't show them that, staying together isn't what's best for them, and it isn't what's best for you, either.

Although it's taken a few years, I can finally say I'm happy. I'm happy with the changes I've made to who I am. I'm also happy in my current relationship. I know Zander thinks he wants his parents together, but I shudder to think about where I'd be now if things hadn't changed.

For me, I was still head over heels in love with my son's father when I left. But becoming a mom changed me, and I started seeing the man I married in a different light. I started seeing his behavior differently, and I realized he was not the kind of man I wanted Zander to have as a role model.

When I started dating again after my divorce, I looked at potential partners as role models for my son. I would ask myself if I would be proud of Zander becoming like this man, and if the answer was no, I would end the relationship.

Growing up, boys want to be like the male role models in their life, and girls want to be like the female role models. I chose a partner through those lenses, and it was also why I tried to become a better person. I knew Zander would someday look for a woman like his mom, and who I was wasn't the type of woman I wanted him to be with.

I told my peer the same thing during a coaching call a few weeks ago. And I also realized I had to be the woman that I was in order to have Zander. A ton of forgiveness came from that realization. For years I wished I had chosen a different man to have a child with. But a different father means I would have had a different child, and I wouldn't change my son for the world.

I say this in hopes of helping you in your struggle. A lot of pain can come from divorce, especially when children are involved. I grew up with divorced parents, but they were great co-parents. I never once saw them argue, and I am grateful for that gift.

My intention for this chapter is not to give relationship advice, but if it is possible to have a cordial relationship with your kids' dad, the benefits for them are tremendous. If you can't have a civil relationship with him (I haven't figured out how to make that happen for me), do yourself a favor and forgive him and yourself. You can't imagine the peace you'll have when you do.

I did this with a tool we call the Total Truth Letter. This tool helps you express and release emotions you feel in your body. My coach says, "Emotions buried alive never die." I believe it's a book too. But once we express them, they are no longer trapped, and we can escape them.

Our emotions have levels: anger, hurt, fear, regret, desires, and love. If there is anger, all other emotions exist as well. If you are angry at your ex (parents, children, friends, boss, and even yourself), write a Total Truth Letter. This is not a letter you need to send to the recipient. It is better if you write the first draft with zero intention of sending it because you won't hold anything back. Don't hold anything back! Expressing emotions releases them.

When writing the Total Truth Letter, complete the following sentences until you feel you've expressed all the feelings behind them:

"I am angry that/when…"

"It hurts me when…"

"I am scared that…"

"I am sorry that…"

"What I really want is…"

"I love and appreciate you for…"

If you resist doing this exercise, it is imperative that you do it! One of my most significant breakthroughs in coaching was writing this letter to myself. I've written it to myself several times for different reasons. A ton of healing comes from writing a letter like this to an ex, your current partner, and even your own parents. I've written a few to my ex and I've finally gotten to a point where I no longer feel resentment toward the past. Just to reiterate, it is extremely powerful if written to anyone you are still holding onto unexpressed emotions towards. If you won't do this for your own healing, do this for your kids. You will be amazed at the outcome, and they deserve it as much as you do.

Good Moms Don't Need Advice

I mentioned in another chapter that I didn't always know I wanted to be a mom. I also mentioned that I didn't ever think about what type of mom I wanted to be until I did it on my own. I was open to suggestions from the "good moms" I knew.

There's no shortage of advice for a new mother. I never counted, but I wouldn't be surprised if, while I was pregnant and had an infant, I received fifty suggestions a day about how to be a parent. "Don't drink coffee." "You can have one cup of coffee a day." "Drink as much coffee as you want." "Sleep when the baby is sleeping." "Don't breastfeed more than or less than a year." I could probably go on, but it's been eleven years since I had a newborn, and I don't recall all of it.

It's natural to want to share your struggles and how you overcame them. That's even the motivation behind this book—sharing my trials with you and how I overcame them.

I was open to the suggestions people gave me. I implemented the ones I agreed with and discarded the ones I didn't. Many people struggle with listening to the suggestions because they feel like the suggestion means you don't know what you're doing or that that person is calling you a bad mom. There was advice I took and some I didn't take. Some people advised me how to get Zander to stop being a picky eater. Their suggestions were not aligned with what I thought was best for him, and because of my relationship with those people, it was more difficult to say no.

One time, I told my brother a way to drop his son off with a sitter that would help avoid meltdowns. My brother's response was, "Thank you for your opinion." And what I heard was, "You don't know what you're talking about."

In that situation, two things were happening. I was angry that he wasn't taking my advice because I knew what I was talking about, and I thought he was saying I didn't. The other piece was that I was jealous that he had the confidence to say, "Thank you for your opinion," and I didn't. With certain people, I still don't.

The Truth

Good moms don't need advice, except when:

- *they want it.*

There are always going to be people giving unsolicited advice. The advice doesn't mean they think negatively about you as a person or a parent; they just care about you enough that they don't want to see you struggle or make a "mistake" like they did. Most of the time, it comes from a good place.

Some people in my life gave me suggestions I disagreed with. Because of my relationship with those people, and my inability to say, "Thank you for your opinion," I asked that they not give me advice unless I asked for it directly. Having those boundaries with people is okay when you don't feel you need advice. Most importantly, it's okay to know when you need advice and when you don't.

If you are receiving unsolicited advice, and it's upsetting you, I want you to know that most of the time, advice is given because the person cares about you and wants to help. Most advice is not given from a place of malice, nor is it only given to people perceived as inept. Receiving and understanding the advice can help heal your relationship.

Some people look down on others and give advice from a place of superiority. Remember, just because advice is offered doesn't mean it must be taken.

Looking back, my parenting approach was to do what I felt was right. When unsure, I would ask for help until I heard the right answer. I recently started working with a parent educator, Melanie Soloway, with nearly 20 years' experience. She's taught me and countless other parents the tools that once seemed like magic to her but realized they were rooted in brain science. I have learned and continue to learn tools to educate moms to help them raise happy, healthy children.

Good Moms Don't Try to Change Their Kids

I interviewed a mom, Teresa, who told me about her guilt for raising her daughter, Sophia, who had grown up to be a lesbian. As Sophia grew, she didn't like wearing dresses and leaned more toward typical boy activities.

Teresa insisted that her daughter wear dresses to church because that is what girls are meant to do. Around the time Sophia turned 18, she confessed to her mom that she was a lesbian. And that's when Teresa's guilt set in. Teresa told me that after Sophia told her who she was, she saw signs of it all along. She struggled to forgive herself every time she forced her daughter to be someone she wasn't. To this day, she still apologizes to Sophia for not allowing her to be her authentic self.

The Truth

Good moms don't try to change their kids, except when:

- *they don't know better.*

In the past twenty years or more, the culture around sexuality and gender identity has changed significantly to a place where people are now more open to discussion. We are beginning to see acceptance of homosexuality and gender fluidity. But at the time Sophia was growing up, homosexuality wasn't socially acceptable and generally not understood. My mom friend judged herself for not knowing what she didn't know.

Throughout the rest of my conversation with Teresa, I heard many of the ways she showed how much she cared for her daughter and the awe-inspiring life lessons she instilled in her, but the thing she focused on most was her mistakes.

This is why guilt isn't serving you, and it's time to let it go. While you judge yourself for the mistakes you made, you're focusing all your energy on what you did wrong and none on what you did right.

We feel guilty because we judge those things as wrong, and we care about our children that we only want what is best for them. But what if what happened was what was best for them? What if everything you've done thus far is exactly what you were supposed to do?

If what you did was wrong, such as the examples I've shared, and you want to make a change, make the changes you feel are best now and move forward. With added information, you can create new choices. Judging yourself for past mistakes doesn't change the past, and it's not compassionate to the "you" you used to be. She got you to where you are.

Self-improvement is part of life. Learning from our mistakes is an incredible blessing we have. Loving yourself along the way is the compassion you deserve and makes changing easier.

Good Moms Don't Lose Connection With Their Kids and Protects Them at All Costs

Written by Melanie Soloway

$\mathcal{B}$ efore becoming a mother, I worked as Deputy District Attorney in Los Angeles County in California. One of my assignments as a prosecutor was in juvenile court where I witnessed firsthand how children made some bad choices. I judged this as the result of them not having good enough connections with their parents and thus not having "good enough parents."

After becoming a mother of twins in 2002, I was determined that this result would not happen in my family, so I dedicated myself to motherhood. I saw it as my job to ensure that I did everything I could to become the "best parent" I could be. Logically, this meant, that I would be able to control the outcome so that my children would turn out to be great kids who would only make "good choices." I quit my job as a prosecutor, and prior to even having my third son during my first three years of motherhood I had taken my parenting skills to what I perceived was the next level. In addition to reading dozens of parenting books and taking several parenting courses and trainings, I subsequently got certified in three different parenting programs. Over the next couple of decades, I started two parent education businesses and taught hundreds of parent tools to ensure they could be the best parents they could be. On the outside, my life looked pretty picture perfect. I was married to a wealthy man, had three children and we owned a home on the beach in Santa Monica, California, and it looked like I was living the American dream.

On the inside, however, behind closed doors, I buried some secrets. My husband had not been faithful, and even when the lies, cheating, and gaslighting escalated we agreed to see a therapist and "work on it." The justification I gave myself was that it was also my job to sacrifice myself and my happiness in a relationship to spare my sons from what I was afraid could harm them. However, in the South African Summer in December 2014, I took my American born husband and children back to my country of birth to introduce them to my roots. Even though Nelson Mandela died a year before we arrived, the legacy and message of love and forgiveness he extended that freed my country of origin was alive and thriving. The experience was so magical I told everyone who would listen, including my husband, that I would write a book about this incredible phenomenon. My husband berated me expressing his opinion that I was not a "good writer." Upon entering the cell, which had been turned into a museum where Nelson Mandela had spent many years of his life, my soul whispered, "It's time to leave this toxic marriage you have stayed in ten years too long." Mr. Mandela's body may have been trapped behind bars for fighting for justice, but they could never trap his mind. I (my soul that is, the inner sense of knowing) knew that while externally it looked like I was living a very free life, I was trapped inside the cells of my own body and programming.

By October 2015, my soul was shaking me out of this marriage I had wanted to leave for so long. The medical condition where my body goes into spasms from stress was flaring so much, I realized the choice I had was to end up divorced or end up in hospital. My husband finally agreed to both the divorce and the plan that the best interests of the children would be paramount.

What happened in the months and years that followed left me feeling like I had entered an alternate universe. My husband used hundreds of thousands of dollars and attacked my motherhood making me the target of parental alienation*. Parental alienation occurs when one parent targets the other and uses strategies like badmouthing and far more subtle ways to "brainwash" the kids so that the children reject the targeted parent. I had never heard of parental alienation. When I retained my second attorney, he gave me the evidence of what parental alienation is and how it is accomplished in a book entitled "Divorce Poison" by Dr. Richard Warshak. The explanation read like a script my husband had followed. This was supported by many YouTube videos that Dr. Craig Childress did on the subject. I could not fathom how the attorneys, charging me north of $675, and having represented me for months, either weren't aware of parental alienation or simply did not inform me of it. My new attorney, who represented A-list movie stars, predicted that this ship had sailed, the damage was done, and there would be no turning things around. Parental Alienation can be accomplished very swiftly, and the children often not only lose their

---

* There is a controversy in the legal arena regarding the term parental alienation because of the Doctor who coined it and the scientific proof he offered, and it has since been called parent estrangement. This dispute continues in legal arenas despite the thousands upon thousands of families and children affected and the books written by adult children about its effects. For any parent who has experienced it, we can assure those in doubt that it exists. The complexities of when it is used as a shield are real too, which does not diminish the damage that is caused when it is used as a weapon.

connection with the targeted parent but the family of that parent too. This occurred with two of my three children. There is a controversy in the legal arena regarding parental alienation, despite the thousands upon thousands of families and children affected and the books written by adult children about its effects. For any parent who has experienced it, we can assure those in doubt that it exists. Despite the odds being stacked against me, I was not prepared to quit. A good mother protects her kids, and despite the hundreds of thousands of dollars it would take, I was unequivocally committed to protecting them "at all costs." In retrospect, I realize I was too stubborn, too programmed, too stupid, too ashamed, and in too much pain. I trusted a system I thought I knew. Unfortunately, despite my valiant commitment and efforts, the American "justice" system did not render justice to me or my children.

Losing the connection to my teens was devastating. Still, in retrospect, having 50% custody of my youngest son saved me from not fully drowning in my sorrow. Despite this, though, I did enter a hole so dark and deep I did not know if I would ever crawl fully back into the light. I spent years in the darkness of pain, focusing on the blame, the guilt, and the shame. However, I continued as the mother martyr because that was my job, my role, or so I believed. And then my youngest began to sink. Covid came, and it was a storm on top of the storm he was already navigating. I thought I was in the boat trying to save him as I spoke to therapists and teachers, doing all I could to throw him the ropes I believed he needed. Eventually, I had to admit that I did not have the solution, and I decided to send my youngest son to a residential program so he could get the help he needed. I felt like a failure, and I knew if I could not save him, I sure as heck would not stand by and watch him drown. The program director went to ask all parents to attend a twelve-step program; any would do.

I went to Al-Anon thinking I did not belong there because my now ex-husband was a workaholic and perhaps a sexaholic but not an alcoholic. I did not comprehend how his father, having been an alcoholic and it being a family disease that carries forward through generations if untreated, was impacting our family. However, as the "good mother," I did what I needed to do to save my son. Simultaneously, as my higher power, the creator, divine source, I call this source God, would have it, I was also directed into a transformational coaching program, and the pull on my soul was so strong I followed the call. The result is that I began the slow crawl out of the darkness and re-found myself. I realized through the work I now do as a neuro-transformational life coach that I had completely lost my identity. I was a "good mother" and a parent educator, and without those two roles and "titles," I was lost at sea. I convinced myself I had failed and was not a "good mother." When I began to "do the work," I realized I was not in a boat throwing ropes to my child; I was in the water, drowning next to him. I have learned that the key to my liberation is through the trinity of the connection triangle - to myself, to others, and to a higher power. When I strengthened all three sides of this triangle, my life began to do a 180-degree turn.

The Truth

The Good mother rule
We all know the one
She would run onto the fire to save her son,
Nothing is off limits for this mother bear, even murder would be an
option if anyone would dare,
To hurt her baby boy
But what if?
What if she did not know the dangers that lurked
Like a cunning, clever fox disguised in the woods
What if the monster that came to take her child
was hideously, insidiously, hiding

like a cancer but not quite so overt
one that morphs in the mind and the body
into the fabric of cells turning into traits that are far more clever
Far less detectable, far more acceptable
A family disease,
Alcoholism
one that spans the generations
gets buried inside the systems
So that when the carrier, a raging alcoholic, committed suicide
decades before the mother even met his spawn
How could she possibly know or understand the ramifications
Of a disease that spreads without limitations
One that has no feelings or concern for the cells it
invades to reside in
So here's the exception,
To the good mother rule
it's when she cannot be
expected to know the unknowable!
Compassion is in order
Not just for the husband, the father who took her child
But compassion for herself to alleviate the pain, the guilt, and the
shame.
Blame, to harbor the feeling, is an option
But holding onto the anger inside her body merely causes her even
more pain that she does not deserve,
and frankly, nor does he
He, the father of her children is the product of that system
When the disease manifests itself in his cells
Because it was passed down through the generations
Ancestral manifestations seep into societal programming labels what
he does is good too

He is the workaholic
a very reputable trait
The provider, the achiever, the guard at the gate
His black hole so deep and so dark that all he wants is love, affection,
and approval for the little boy inside of him
His inner child who was neglected, abused, and abandoned,
He, too, does not know how to heal the wounds of his past
And without getting the help to break the chains
he does not fully grasp
He perpetuates them into his future
And the good mother is blindsided by the disease she does not see
coming
The disease she did not cause, cannot cure or control
The disease that rips her family apart
That was there from the start
But she did not know!

Working through my guilt, shame, and self-blame has not been easy. However, the payoff has undoubtedly begun to reveal itself. Almost five years after being estranged from my twins, one of them reached out. I then had contact with both of my twins. Although I know the road ahead will not be straight, I have faith that whatever lessons are meant to show up, not just for me but for us all, are here for our growth. If we choose to learn from them, we will grow.

I am learning to trust that the journey of motherhood and, more importantly, life is not about some phantom destination. Life is replete with storms; the only way to survive them is to keep riding the waves. More importantly, the only way to thrive from them is to enjoy the ride! There is no such thing as a perfect child; from my perspective, there is only one perfect parent. Although I was born into and told what religion I belong to, I know there is only one perfect parent; for me, the name I give to this perfect parent and my higher power is God. I am not a particularly religious, and I am building my relationship with this entity. However, I know that my soul arrived in my container, and the life experiences I am learning will help me evolve. It requires an enlightened parent to raise an enlightened child. I create harmony by aligning my thoughts, words, and actions with my heart. In the healing, I found forgiveness, not just for my ex-husband but in forgiving myself. I eventually applied the lessons I learned from Nelson Mandela many years before.

It was through forgiving myself, my S.O.U.L., state of unconditional love, that I found the exception to the rule for when a good mother does not lose connection with her children and protects them at all costs. We cannot know what we do not know. We can always only do the best we can with what we know at any given point in time. My job as a mother is to love my children just as God loves them, and God loves me. It is also to care enough to make decisions and take actions that align at any given moment and then to trust. If I make a wrong turn, I have faith that I will be guided to pivot. Now I just have to work on being the best version of myself and make whatever changes are necessary to be the person I want my children to see.

As a neuro-transformational life coach, in addition to my expertise and experience as a parent educator, I am committed to helping other mothers and fathers who are struggling despite their best efforts to be the best parents they can be. The truth is that children do what we do and not what we say. Therefore, the best way to help our kids begins with helping ourselves. I can be reached at melanie@ raisingenlightenedchildren.com and would love to hear from you if you want or need support as you navigate your parenting journey.

Good Moms Don't Get Sad

⸺⸺◦⸙◦⸺⸺

T his chapter was the most difficult to write, and I also felt I needed to save it for last. It's different because I will tell you about a little self-discovery I made while resisting writing it. I even considered taking it out of the book. "Moms don't get sad. I don't need to write this chapter."

At the end of 2018, I joined a program to help market myself as a coach. To kick off the program, there was a live event that I planned on attending, but a family emergency pulled me away. I needed clarity on the type of people I wanted to help. A few months later, I attended another event and realized I wanted to help moms. But as soon as I left the event, I was pulled in another direction, and coaching was put on the back burner.

In August 2019, my life coach helped me overcome my guilt for letting Zander get hurt. When I let go of that guilt, the changes I noticed in many areas of my life were too many to count. My passion for helping moms was no longer something I could ignore.

This book essentially began writing itself—until this chapter.

In all my time working with a life coach (at least two years), I never talked about my mom. I didn't have issues with my mom. We have a wonderful relationship. I love talking to her, being with her, and helping her whenever possible. At one point, I noticed I never talked about her with my coach, and I believe I even said I didn't want to because "I was afraid to poke the bear." In other words, I didn't have any conscious bad memories of my mom, and if there were, I didn't want to bring them up. I was happy with the status quo.

Something I noticed about my relationship with her was that I was always her defender. I would defend her to the death if necessary. My mom was a teacher and I remember I wanted to beat up a sixth grader when I was in ninth grade because he was such a thorn in her side. I never blamed my mom for anything, but I was more than happy to blame others until I learned to take responsibility.

Looking back at being a kid, I always knew my mom was sad. I couldn't explain why, but I always knew she was. As an adult, I still don't know why; I just wish she wasn't. I am so passionate about helping moms be happy because, if I could have one wish granted, I would wish for my mom to be happy. That was my response to a question a peer coach asked me.

I realized that, at some point in my childhood, I decided that I was the reason my mom was sad. There was something about me that wasn't good enough because if I were good enough, she would have been happy. And I spent most of my life wanting and trying to be good enough. But I couldn't be the solution since I wasn't the problem.

I decided to write this chapter from the perspective of an adult who grew up with a sad mom. If something keeps you from experiencing your best life, you owe it to yourself and your kids to figure out what it is and how to let it go because we will never know how our actions affect our children.

I know that you want to be the best mom possible because you know that your kids deserve the best. I know that because you wouldn't be reading this book if you didn't. You wouldn't feel guilty. But our brains are not wired to keep us happy or to reach our full potential. Our brains are wired to keep us safe, and in my case, with my son, my brain kept me safe to protect me from the future resentment I thought Zander would feel for me not protecting him.

I am here to tell you that there is hope. With the proper support, you can be happy. If someone had told me what I would get out of hiring a life coach, I would have done it sooner and paid significantly more for it.

I thank you for taking the time to read this book. I honor the time you invested in yourself, and I genuinely hope you found some value in it. If you would like individual support for your struggles, please get in touch with me for a free coaching session. I want to help you see what is possible for your happiness and support you on the journey to becoming the best version of yourself.

Increase Your P.E.A.C.E.

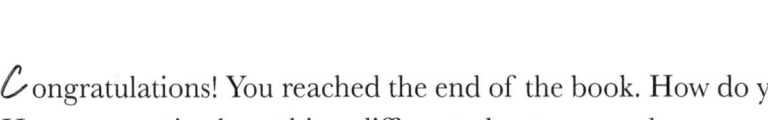

$\mathcal{C}$ongratulations! You reached the end of the book. How do you feel? Have you noticed anything different about you or how you react to things? If not, that's okay. Start paying attention to the differences in how you feel or act, even if they are subtle. You need to acknowledge the changes, or you may slip back into old guilt patterns.

So, you've finished the book...now what?

I would like to encourage you to connect with me and my community of moms. I created a Facebook group called The Imperfect Mom Community. You'll find a supportive community of moms who have struggled with guilt in the past and want support for the future.

If you are looking for more individualized support, I am the Mom Support Coach and would be happy to discuss your specific struggles with you. Just before writing this, I realized that having a coach is something successful people have been doing for a long time. Only recently has it become more mainstream. Humans are not programmed to get the most out of themselves.

If you want to get the most out of your experience on this planet, get a coach! The link to my online coaching calendar can be found on my website: www.alysialyons.com/coaching

Guilt is just one of the emotions that steal our peace as moms. I once posted on Facebook, "What things steal your peace?" I received a wide variety of answers. I took those answers and put them into the following five categories which we need to look at and address to increase our P.E.A.C.E.:

People – We have many relationships with many different people in our lives. People are complicated. Knowing how to create healthy relationships with the people in your life can be difficult.

Emotions – Guilt is one of the many emotions we feel daily. Most of us were not taught the proper way to express them. Some people are afraid to feel at all. I've often heard, "If I allow myself to cry, I'll never stop."

Assets – This word means different things to different people. It could be money, physical things in your home, or something totally different.

Chaos – This can also mean different things to different people. Some people love routine and can't seem to find it. Others thrive in chaos. If your calendar is out of control, that's what I call chaos.

Exhaustion – The short answer is self-care. Self-care and exhaustion mean different things to different people. The important thing is that you are doing something to care for yourself.

I post weekly blogs and podcasts covering each of these topics. I also offer free P.E.A.C.E. assessments to help you discover which areas are stealing your peace and what you can do to change it. Schedule your assessment on alysialyons.com/peace

I hope you've found this book valuable. My sincerest wish is that you live the life you were put on Earth to live and that you find joy in the journey.

Tools & Resources to Help You

Total Truth Letter

The Total Truth Letter is a tool to express buried emotions. This tool is best used without the intention of sending it to the subject of the letter. Don't hold back. Express every emotion until you feel you've released and expressed them all.

"I am angry that/when..."

"It hurts me when..."

"I am scared that..."

"I am sorry that..."

"What I really want is..."

"I love and appreciate you for…

Identify and Clarify Your Values

This is a partner exercise. You can do this with anyone you trust and won't filter for.

Have them ask you, "What's important to you?"

Ask them to repeat this question until you feel complete.

After you have your list of values, rank them by having your partner ask, "What is more important to you, A or B?" If "A" wins, then your partner will ask, "What is more important to you, A or C?"

Have your partner continue through the list until you've gone through your values. If "C" is more important than "A," your partner will then ask, "What is more important, C or D?"

Once you complete the list, you will repeat the process until you have a list of your priorities ranked in order of importance.

Guilt & Shame Exercise

This book is based on releasing guilt and shame, and this tool is used throughout. First, identify the rule you're breaking. As mentioned before, it can be a rule from any of your roles in which you want to feel like a good person. Once you've identified the rule, what is the exception to the broken rule? Even in the legal system, there's an exception to breaking laws. It's against the law to murder someone, but the exception is when someone tries to harm you or others. Finding your exception to the rule you broke may be difficult, but it's there. Don't stop until you find it.

Join a Supportive Community

It takes a village to raise a child, but our culture today is becoming more and more independent from others. Find a supportive community of parents to bounce ideas off of, to vent to, to babysit swap, and other great ideas that you don't have access to with your current awareness.

You can join our online community on Facebook: The Imperfect Mom Community.

Books Referenced

I mentioned a few books above. I wanted to list them here and why I recommend them. If you're looking for your next great read, I recommend the following:

- Rachel Hollis, *Girl, Wash Your Face*
- Rachel Hollis, *Girl, Stop Apologizing*

A friend recommended *Girl, Wash Your Face* a few years ago. In fact, she said she wanted to buy multiple copies of this book to give to random women she met on the street because it made such an impact on her. Rachel's books are inspiring to me. There are few books I read a second time, but I read both books twice.

- Gary Chapman, *The Five Love Languages*

This book has had a profound impact on my life. I learned about it a decade ago, and reading it helped me understand people better. Learning the love languages of those around me has helped me give and receive love more effectively and deepened my relationships with those who are significant to me. One of the most impactful was when I asked Zander his love language.

- Pam Grout, *Thank and Grow Rich*

Most people have heard of the book Think and Grow Rich by Napoleon Hill. I still haven't read it, but I found it on Audible. I have listened to this book more than once. The first time didn't have the lasting impact it did on me the second time. Since rereading it, I have been part of her AA 2.0, and I've seen dramatic changes in my attitude. There are only two steps in AA 2.0. Step 1: Wake up every morning, and before you get out of bed, decide it will be a wonderful day. Step 2: Text someone three things you are grateful for every day. Three new things for which you are grateful. The more you look for things to be grateful for, the more things you have to be grateful for. Don't believe me? Try it for a month and see what happens in your life. And don't forget to read the book.

- Daniel J. Siegel, M.D. and Tina Payne Bryson, PH.D *No-Drama Discipline: The Whole-Brain Way to Calm the Chaos and Nurture Your Child's Developing Mind*

I found this book at a time when I struggled with discipline. Zander had a lot of tantrums when he didn't get his way, and I wanted to learn how to discipline without the drama. Discipline is not a four-letter word. It is something all children need. People often confuse discipline with spanking. This book explains other options to help children learn the lessons, which is the ultimate goal of discipline.

- Harville Hendrix and Helen LaKelly Hunt, *Getting the Love You Want*

This book was recommended to me by my fiancé before we started dating. It was irritating to me because I wanted to be in a relationship with him, and he, well, didn't. Why did he recommend I read a relationship book? It only took me a day and a half to listen to it on Audible. I was addicted. We frequently discuss this book, and whether you're in a relationship, not in a relationship, your relationship is rocky, or it couldn't be better, read or listen to this book!

- Jen Sincero, *You Are a Badass: How to Stop Doubting Your Greatness and Start Living an Awesome Life*

I know I didn't mention this book or her other Badass series books (she just announced a new one being released in December 2020), but while I'm recommending books, this is another must-read. If I had to choose between Jen and Rachel, I don't think I could. The Badass books are exactly that. Bad. Ass.

I hope you find this list helpful. Each of these books and working with a personal life coach has shaped my life into one I love and am profoundly grateful for. If you had asked me seven years ago if I thought I could live a peaceful life, I wouldn't have believed it. I want this for you, too.

- Dr. Richard Warshak, *Divorce Poison*

This is the book Melanie Soloway read during her divorce and devoured it in one evening. I have not read it, but it's a good way to understand exactly what parent alienation is and how damaging it can be to your children.

About the Author

*A*lysia Lyons is a Master Neurotransformation Results Coach, the Co-Director of Raising Enlightened Children, an author, and a podcast host. She is passionate about helping moms become the CEOs of their homes and lives, guiding them to find more joy from the inside out.

As the proud mother of a son who has been the course corrector for her own life, she now leads the parents she works with through long-lasting neurological shifts to help ease their guilt and increase their emotional peace to find their happy.

www.ingramcontent.com/pod-product-compliance
Lightning Source LLC
Chambersburg PA
CBHW071201120626
46546CB00006B/2364